Overcoming Employment Barri

127 Great Tips for Bu...lgs and Finding a Job Tha...ight for You

Second Edition

Ronald L. Krannich, Ph.D.

IMPACT PUBLICATIONS
Manassas Park, VA

ISBNs: 978-1-57023-387-6 (paperback); 978-1-57023-379-1 (eBook)

Library of Congress: 2015919727

Publisher: For information on Impact Publications, including current and forthcoming publications, authors, press kits, online bookstore, newsletters, downloadable catalogs, and submission requirements, visit the left navigation bar on the front page of the main company website: www.impactpublications.com.

Publicity/Rights: For information on publicity, author interviews, and subsidiary rights, contact the Media Relations Department: Tel. 703-361-7300, Fax 703-335-9486, or email: query@impactpublications.com.

Sales/Distribution: All distribution and special sales inquiries should be directed to the publisher: Sales Department, IMPACT PUBLICATIONS, 9104 Manassas Drive, Suite N, Manassas Park, VA 20111-5211, Tel. 703-361-7300, Fax 703-335-9486, or email: query@impactpublications.com. All bookstore and eBook sales are handled through Impact's trade distributor: National Book Network, 15200 NBN Way, Blue Ridge Summit, PA 17214, Tel. 1-800-462-6420.

Quantity Discounts: We offer quantity discounts on bulk purchases. Please review our discount schedule for this book at www.impactpublications.com or contact the Special Sales Department, Tel. 703-361-0255.

The Author: Ronald L. Krannich, Ph.D., is one of today's leading career and travel writers who has authored more than 100 books, including several self-help guides for people in transition and those with not-so-hot backgrounds. A former Peace Corps Volunteer, Fulbright Scholar, and university professor, Ron specializes in producing and distributing books, DVDs, training programs, and related materials on employment, career transition, addiction, anger management, criminal justice, life skills, and travel. He can be contacted at ron@impactpublications.com.

Contents

Index to Barriers

CHAPTER 9 – Salary, Benefits, Offers, and Follow-Up

Selected Books by Author

99 Days to Re-Entry Success Journal
201 Dynamite Job Search Letters
America's Top Internet Job Sites
America's Top Jobs for People Re-Entering the Workforce
The Anger Management Pocket Guide
Best Jobs for Ex-Offenders
Best Jobs for the 21st Century
Best Resumes and Letters for Ex-Offenders
Blue-Collar Resume and Job Hunting Guide
Change Your Job, Change Your Life
The Complete Guide to International Jobs and Careers
The Complete Guide to Public Employment
Dynamite Cover Letters
Dynamite Resumes
The Ex-Offender's 30/30 Job Solution
The Ex-Offender's Job Interview Guide
The Ex-Offender's Quick Job Hunting Guide
The Ex-Offender's Re-Entry Success Guide
Get a Raise in 7 Days
Give Me More Money!
High Impact Resumes and Letters
I Can't Believe They Asked Me That!
I Want to Do Something Else, But I'm Not Sure What It Is
Interview for Success
Job Hunting Tips for People With Hot and Not-So-Hot Backgrounds
Job Interview Tips for People With Not-So-Hot Backgrounds
Jobs for Travel Lovers
Military-to-Civilian Resumes and Letters
Military-to-Civilian Success for Veterans and Their Family
The Military-to-Civilian Transition Pocket Guide
Moving Out of Education
Nail the Cover Letter!
Nail the Resume!
No One Will Hire Me!
Quick Job Finding Pocket Guide
The Re-Entry Employment and Life Skills Pocket Guide
The Re-Entry Personal Finance Pocket Guide
The Re-Entry Start-Up Pocket Guide
Savvy Interviewing
Savvy Networker
Savvy Resume Writer
You Should Hire Me!

1

Turn Employment Barriers Into New Opportunities

"It may be time to re-examine your approach to finding a job. What are you doing that's right and/or wrong? What changes do you need to make? "

WE ALL FACE BARRIERS to getting ahead in life. While some are more challenging than others, most barriers can be overcome through renewed understanding, purpose, determination, and drive. In the case of employment barriers, start by re-examining and resetting your attitudes and mindset – move from "can't do" to "can do" thinking. By so doing, you'll begin seeing what it is you need to do to land a job that's right for you. That's what this book is all about – renewing your approach to finding a job.

Lessons Learned

Leading a curious and inquisitive life results in many "lessons learned." And one important lesson I've learned in working with thousands of job seekers is this: they are often their own worst enemy. Few are victims of a difficult job market, mean employers, or bad luck. Many engage in self-fulfilling prophesies and thus become victims of their own misinformation, poor choices, bad habits, job-stopping red flags, and difficult personalities. Above all, they lack **resilience**, the key to long-term success.

After experiencing a few rejections, many such job seekers lament that "no one will hire me" for a variety of reasons that have nothing to do with their ability to conduct a thoughtful job search campaign.

Expressing the 4Ds of job search failure – **d**iscouraged, **d**isillusioned, **d**epressed, and **d**esperate – they often lack the necessary skills (resume, networking, social media, interviewing, follow up) to clearly communicate their qualifications to employers. In the end, they land jobs that aren't right for them. Not surprisingly, they join the world of many unhappy and unstable workers.

You Must Take Charge of Your Future

You have to work at making things happen for you. Indeed, each day thousands of people encounter physical, mental, emotional, relational, career, and financial barriers that once seemed impossible to overcome. Purpose-driven, motivated, and persistent, many people decide to take charge of their fate and future by turning barriers into challenges and opportunities. They learn how to transform their lives by making smart decisions about their future. They have dreams that direct them into the future rather than a litany of obstacles that keep them wedded to the negative past. For them, life may at times be unfair and tough, but it also can be very good.

Overcoming Self-Imposed Barriers

While many people encounter barriers to achieving goals, few barriers are ever insurmountable. Most pose challenges that require a positive attitude and purposeful strategies for success. As many people quickly discover, if you do nothing, you get nothing; if you are negative, you attract negative outcomes. Indeed, for most people, their major barrier is found within themselves – the unwillingness to take the necessary actions to change their life for the better. Some learn to get over themselves and focus on what's really important to them. Shedding self-imposed barriers, they go on to shape a life they really love. This should be your goal as you attempt to overcome self-imposed barriers to employment.

For most people, their major barrier is found within themselves – the unwillingness to take the necessary actions to change their life.

Change, whether it's voluntary or forced, is not always welcomed. If, for example, you lost your job, chances are you went through Kubler-

Ross's classic five stages of death and dying or loss and grief – denial, anger, bargaining, depression, and acceptance. But change is often beneficial because it refocuses and re-energizes our lives. It allows us to go on to develop new skills and fulfill new dreams. Upon reflection years later, many people admit losing their job was one of the best things that ever happened to them! But experiencing the process was anything but rewarding.

Hot and Not-So-Hot People

Why are some people more successful in finding jobs and pursuing attractive careers than others? What do they know and do that's different from other less successful people? Are they more intelligent, knowledgeable, skilled, and entrepreneurial? Perhaps they have better connections, work harder, and communicate well with employers. Some may get breaks because of their age, gender, race, class, religion, or political affiliation. Or maybe they are just luckier then others – they always seem to be in the right place at the right time. They get promoted, enjoy great compensation, and always seem to be "in demand" by other employers who want to hire these stars.

We seem to know a lot about less successful people, and especially those with not-so-hot backgrounds who fail to excel according to our expectations. They often lack knowledge and essential education and workplace skills, express negative attitudes, fail to demonstrate good work and workplace habits, communicate poorly, engage in addictive behaviors (drugs, alcohol, and tobacco), live dysfunctional lives, get into trouble both on and off the job, and frequently change jobs or get fired. Some may be discriminated against because of their age, gender, race, or disability. And some have bad luck related to their health, family, or finances. Some face numerous barriers to employment that are difficult to overcome despite their best intentions and efforts.

Making Smart Decisions Again and Again

Over the years I've observed one other important factor that explains job and career success – the ability of some individuals to repeatedly make smart career moves. Most people have at some time during their lives faced barriers to employment. Perhaps you wanted to pursue a certain educational or training program, but you couldn't afford the costs, didn't make the grade, or quit the program. Do you remember being rejected for a job you really wanted? Perhaps you lacked the necessary qualifications or your competition did much better in the job interview.

Have you ever been surprised about the outcome of a job you thought you would really love? Perhaps you weren't promoted, associated with the wrong people, said the wrong things, stayed around too long with a declining organization, saw your job get outsourced or offshored, and thus you got laid off or fired. When you tried looking for another job, you initially felt depressed because no one wanted to hire you – you seemed too old, too expensive, or over-qualified. Maybe it was time to consider a career change. You understood there were certain barriers to employment you needed to overcome if you were to continue on your path to career success.

Overcoming Your Barriers

Much of success in life is all about taking personal responsibility for your choices as well as making smart decisions. While some people lack opportunities because of fundamental choices or circumstances beyond their control – live in a community with few well-paying jobs or experience chronic illnesses that prevent them from holding a job – most people have the power to make choices that can improve their employability, income, and relationships. They regularly make decisions about their education and training, spending patterns, eating and drinking habits, and personal relationships. All of these decisions have **consequences**.

> *Dysfunctional individuals frequently make decisions that have disastrous outcomes in several areas of their lives.*

But the outcomes of individual choices vary greatly. Some people live extremely dysfunctional lives whereas others seem to be successful at everything they do. Many people regularly spend more money than they make, live from paycheck to paycheck, incur debilitating credit card debts, work in dead-end jobs, lack good workplace habits, frequently lose their jobs, neglect their families, experience failed relationships, engage in unhealthy behaviors, express anger publicly, become violent, or have run-ins with the criminal justice system. Such individuals soon become "risky business" for employers, who prefer hiring people they can trust to work in the best interests of the company.

Habits – both good and bad – form early in life and are difficult to change. Successful and resilient people often take risks that repeatedly result in positive outcomes. On the other hand, dysfunctional individuals, who often exhibit co-occurring disorders or multiple negative behaviors (substance abuse, anger, depression), frequently make decisions that have disastrous outcomes in several areas of their lives – from employment and consumption to family relations and public behavior. Accumulating numerous red flags that define their not-so-hot backgrounds, many of these people simply don't understand how, nor are they sufficiently motivated, to make good decisions that result in positive outcomes for themselves and others around them. These losers make a habit of failure rather than a habit of success. Only major cognitive therapy that focuses on changing individual decision-making seems to have a positive impact on such individuals. If you run with dysfunctional people, you, too, may become a loser in the game of life.

What do successful job seekers do that separates them from their less successful counterparts? What critical choices do they make? How do they approach their job search, communicate with potential employers, complete applications, market their resumes and letters, and follow through to get job interviews? Are there some simple tips and strategies you can acquire from them that will enhance your own job search communication and employability? What can we learn from such successful job seekers?

What Are Barriers to Employment?

Barriers to employment are roadblocks on the highway of life. They are roadblocks that can prevent you from getting a job you want, keeping a job, or being promoted from the job you have. The potential barriers to finding and keeping a job are considerable, and may be created by a wide variety of causes. Some barriers may result from behaviors that you, as an individual, have control over, such as attitudes or work habits. Other barriers may be the result of the circumstances you find yourself in, such as living in a job-scarce area where jobs are disappearing rather than being created. Whether the roadblocks you face result from actions within your control, or result from something seemingly beyond your control, such as where you were born and happen to live, most barriers do not have to be permanent.

Most barriers, like the roadblocks on the highway, can be left in place, or either moved or removed completely. To do something or to do nothing – these are choices we make. Doing nothing is just as much an option as deciding to take action and make changes. Leaving barriers in place and doing nothing about them may sometimes seem to be

> *Red flags are things that alert a future employer to the potholes in your life.*

the easiest option. But as we stay put, we are forced to continually confront the barrier and stay in place, going nowhere. Some roadblocks are easier and take less time to get rid of than others, but each can be dealt with. Fixing the highway so the roadblocks can be removed may be relatively easy if the potholes are few and not very big. It will take more of our time and attention if the potholes are numerous or deep. But the rewards of recognizing and fixing the potholes to smooth out the highway are great. So let's get started!

Red Flags Alert Employers to the Potholes

What do I mean by "red flags"? Red flags are things that alert a future (or your present) employer to the potholes in your life. For example, your behavior in the job interview may raise a red flag, or something you put on your resume, or information omitted on your resume may raise a red flag in the employer's mind. Let's take a quick look at some examples so you'll have a better understanding of what I mean. I'll come back and revisit these examples in more depth later.

Let's start with your resume. It briefly outlines six different jobs and employers in the past four years. This may tell the interviewer, who looks for **patterns and potential red flags**, that you are a serial job hopper. You either don't or can't hold a job for very long. If this employer hires you, you probably won't be around here very long either. That means you're likely to leave or the employer will have to fire you after a few weeks or months on the job, and the employer will be left with a vacancy to fill and the need to train yet another person for the job. That costs the employer time and money. A **big** red flag.

Maybe it's not something you put on your resume, but something you left off or said. The employer sees you have apparent gaps in your employment history. There are significant periods of time for which you have not indicated what you were doing. The employer is left to wonder what you are hiding. You must be hiding something or you would have indicated on your resume what you were doing for that time period. Another **big** red flag. Or you arrive late for your job interview, raising a red flag in front of the interviewer's eyes. If you can't even be on time for the job interview, how can he expect you'll be on time for work everyday? Give the interviewer a lame excuse for being late – his or her directions weren't clear – and you and your red flags just went up in flames!

If you recognize yourself in any of these scenarios, you have potholes in your life. You are a job hopper – that's a red flag that indicates a pothole. You have periods of time during which you apparently don't want the employer to know what you were doing – red flag, pothole. You are late for the job interview – red flag, pothole.

Each of the potholes is a **barrier**. The red flags simply **alert** the employer to the existence of the potholes. To overcome the barriers that get in the way of your employment, you must first recognize the pothole (barrier), and the reason this is a concern to an employer (red flag), and then repair the pothole to remove the barrier and smooth out your career highway.

> *Until you admit and take responsibility for your barriers, you're not going to make the necessary changes.*

Caution Signals, Detours, and Road Closed Ahead

As you encounter the potholes that I identify, you will no doubt see yourself in some, but certainly not all of them. The first step is to recognize you have a pothole that needs fixing. Until you admit to yourself that you have a problem, and take responsibility for it, you're not going to take any steps to fix it. And in fact, if you ignore the problem, chances are you will keep digging the hole deeper and deeper. Once you recognize what the problem is and resolve to fix it, you can begin to repair the damage.

This book is organized to help you recognize the potholes that are barriers to getting or keeping the job you want. It discusses each barrier to help you understand why it is a red flag to employers. Finally, it provides tips to help you repair the pothole and remove the barrier so you can get on with a better work life.

In some cases your pothole just has a caution sign next to it. If, for example, you continue to change jobs as frequently as you have in the past, it will raise a red flag to future employers. But for now you just have a yellow flashing caution light. If you change the negative behavior now, it need never become a pothole.

Other potholes may suggest a change of course. If you lack skills or training for a job you want, you may need to make a detour and acquire the necessary skills to be considered for the job. That detour may take some time, but you can do it!

Occasionally the road ahead may be closed. If you have a criminal record and have been convicted of a felony, there are certain jobs that by law you simply will not be able to hold. If that is the case, a change of goals may be necessary. Whatever your situation, whether you face a caution signal, a detour, or a "road closed ahead" sign, it is still possible to repair the potholes and drive off on a smoother, but perhaps different, road ahead.

Ask Others for Assistance If Necessary

You'll probably identify with many of the employment barriers outlined in this book as well as know what actions you need to take in order to overcome those barriers. If you're not sure what to do next, you may want to seek assistance from others. In fact, you are well advised to seek professional career advice when it comes time to complete various steps in the job search process, such as assessing their skills, getting goals, writing resumes, and preparing for the job interview. When that time comes, you should contact personnel at your local American Job Center (jobcenter.usa.gov). You also can hire a career coach and/or professional resume writer to help you with your job search. Begin with:

- **Professional Association of Resume Writers and Career Coaches**   www.parw.com
- **National Resume Writers' Association**   www.thenrwa.com
- **Career Directors International**   careerdirectors.com
- **International Coach Federation**   www.internationalcoach federation.com

2

Test Your Employment Barriers I.Q.

"How many barriers are you likely to encounter when looking for employment?"

IT WOULD BE GREAT IF we could instantly identify our employment barriers and then make the necessary changes so we could thrive in today's job market and workplace. It's not that easy, but at least you can start moving in that direction by completing this and subsequent chapters, which attempt to help you identify, analyze, and overcome 127 barriers to employment outlined in this book.

How effective are you in finding a job? What barriers are you most likely to face in getting ahead in your career? Which barriers can you quickly overcome by changing your approach to today's job market and workplace?

Take the Test

These and many other barriers to employment questions are addressed in the following quiz:

INSTRUCTIONS: Respond to each statement by circling which number at the right best represents your situation.

SCALE: 1 = Strongly agree   4 = Disagree
2 = Agree   5 = Strongly disagree
3 = Maybe, not certain

Skills and Work History

1. I have a strong educational background related
   to the work I want to do.   1 2 3 4 5

2. I have an excellent work record.   1 2 3 4 5

3. My references will give me excellent recommendations.   1 2 3 4 5

4. I usually stay with an employer for at least three years.   1 2 3 4 5

5. I have appropriate technological skills for the work I want to do.   1 2 3 4 5

6. I have a good command of the English language.   1 2 3 4 5

Attitudes and Behaviors

7. I do not have addictions related to drugs, alcohol, or gambling.   1 2 3 4 5

8. I usually take responsibility for my own actions rather than blame other people for my situation or circumstance.   1 2 3 4 5

9. I'm a very honest person who tries to do the right thing.   1 2 3 4 5

10. Most employers find me dependable and trustworthy.   1 2 3 4 5

11. I am generally a very positive person who avoids saying negative things about others.   1 2 3 4 5

12. I'm a very tolerant person who welcomes differing points of view.   1 2 3 4 5

13. I seldom get angry or exhibit a temper.   1 2 3 4 5

14. I don't brag about myself to others.   1 2 3 4 5

15. I'm very good with small talk.   1 2 3 4 5

16. I've very polite and respectful of others.   1 2 3 4 5

17. I'm very entrepreneurial.   1 2 3 4 5

18. I'm sensitive to others and try to be considerate.   1 2 3 4 5

19. I tend to project a very positive image through what I wear and say.   1 2 3 4 5

20. I'm more extroverted than introverted.   1 2 3 4 5

Health, Wellness, and Disabilities

21. I'm generally a very healthy person who both feels and looks healthy.   1 2 3 4 5

22. I watch my diet and regularly exercise.   1 2 3 4 5

23. I don't have mental health issues, such as depression, bipolar disorder, paranoia, or others.   1 2 3 4 5

24. I don't have a physical disability that would negatively affect my work.   1 2 3 4 5

25. I seldom miss work because of illness.   1 2 3 4 5

26. I have very good personal hygiene habits.   1 2 3 4 5

27. I tend to look younger than my age.   1 2 3 4 5

28. I'm usually very energetic and enthusiastic.   1 2 3 4 5

Prerequisites for Success

29. I'm relatively debt free.   1 2 3 4 5

30. I have few red flags in my background that would be barriers to employment.   1 2 3 4 5

31. I've never been fired.   1 2 3 4 5

32. I've never been convicted of a crime.   1 2 3 4 5

33. I have regular access to the Internet.   1 2 3 4 5

34. I have few personal issues that would interfere with my work.   1 2 3 4 5

35. I have all the documents (birth certificate, Social Security number, driver's license, professional licenses, and certificates) I need to qualify for employment.   1 2 3 4 5

36. I know how to organize and implement an effective job search.   1 2 3 4 5

37. I'm very realistic about how much time and work it will take to find a job.   1 2 3 4 5

38. I handle rejections very well.   1 2 3 4 5

39. I have lots of good ideas I would like to share with employers.   1 2 3 4 5

40. I can pass a thorough background check with flying colors.   1 2 3 4 5

41. I usually watch what I say to others.   1 2 3 4 5

42. I'm prepared to deal with any objections to my candidacy.   1 2 3 4 5

43. I understand how to use job fairs to my advantage.   1 2 3 4 5

44. I know where to turn for professional job search assistance.   1 2 3 4 5

45. I tend to be very articulate.   1 2 3 4 5

Finding a Job

46. I know what motivates me to excel at work.   1 2 3 4 5

47. I can identify my strongest abilities and skills.   1 2 3 4 5

48. I can talk about five major achievements that clarify a pattern of interests and abilities that are relevant to my job and career.   1 2 3 4 5

49. I know what I both like and dislike in work.   1 2 3 4 5

50. I have a well defined career objective that focuses my job search on particular organizations and employers.   1 2 3 4 5

51. I know what skills I can offer employers in different occupations.   1 2 3 4 5

52. I know what skills employers most seek in candidates.   1 2 3 4 5

53. I can clearly explain to employers what I do well and enjoy doing.   1 2 3 4 5

54. I can specify why employers should hire me.   1 2 3 4 5

55. I can gain the support of family and friends for making a job or career change.   1 2 3 4 5

56. I can find 10 to 20 hours a week to conduct a part-time job search.   1 2 3 4 5

57. I have the financial ability to sustain a three-month job search.   1 2 3 4 5

58. I can conduct library and Internet research on different occupations, employers, organizations, and communities.   1 2 3 4 5

59. I know how to best use social media to brand myself and connect with employers.   1 2 3 4 5

60. I have an attractive LinkedIn profile.   1 2 3 4 5

61. I can write different types of effective resumes and job search/thank-you letters.   1 2 3 4 5

62. I know where to find outstanding professional resume writers and career coaches.   1 2 3 4 5

63. I can produce and distribute resumes and letters to the right people.   1 2 3 4 5

64. I can list my major accomplishments in action terms.   1 2 3 4 5

65. I can identify and target employers I want to interview.   1 2 3 4 5

66. I know which websites are best for posting resumes and browsing job postings.   1 2 3 4 5

67. I know how much of my time I should spend conducting an online job search.   1 2 3 4 5

68. I can develop a job referral network.   1 2 3 4 5

69. I can persuade others to join in forming a job search support group.   1 2 3 4 5

70. I can prospect for job leads.   1 2 3 4 5

71. I have a very pleasant telephone voice.   1 2 3 4 5

TOTAL [   ]

Calculate your overall ability to overcome employment barriers by adding the numbers you circled for a composite score. If your total is more than 200 points, you face several barriers to employment that you need to work on changing. How you scored each item will indicate to what degree you need to work on overcoming various barriers. The following chapters will help you overcome most of these barriers. If your score is under 130 points, you are well on your way toward employment success!

And Re-Take the Test

After completing this book, you should take this text over again to see if your score has significantly changed. Keep knocking down those barriers that continue to affect your employability. Continue re-taking this test periodically until you score under 130 points.

PART II

Employment Red Flags
That May Change

3

Skills and Work History
as Barriers

---

*"Employers look for candidates who can demonstrate that they can do the job well. They want **evidence** of skills and **proof of performance** rather than mere understanding of assigned duties and responsibilities."*

L ET'S START BY LOOKING AT red flags that relate to your preparation for the job, because lack of preparation will usually take some time to repair. From the perspective of employers, these are key barriers to employment.

BARRIER #1
Lack adequate or appropriate education

QUESTIONS: Do you lack the educational background employers expect applicants who apply for this job to have? Do you wish you had a better education or could acquire more training?

IF YES: There are certain minimum educational requirements employers expect applicants to have when they apply for a specific position. These requirements vary according to the job, but often, at the very least, require a high school diploma (or GED). Although a high school diploma is not required for every job, it becomes more essential as time goes on. Additional education (college) or training (vocational) beyond a high school diploma is required for entry to many jobs as well as advancement once in the position.

TIPS: An obvious solution is to get the necessary education. You'll find numerous education opportunities available through high school adult education programs, vocational and business schools, community colleges, workforce development programs, churches, community groups, nonprofit organizations, colleges, and universities. Some programs are free, others are responsibly priced, and still others are very expensive. For information on education and training programs near your community, be sure to visit the following websites sponsored by the federal government:

- **AmericanJobCenter** jobcenter.usa.gov/education-and-training
- **CareerOneStop**   www.careeronestop.org/toolkit/toolkit.aspx

You'll find numerous online education and training programs (distance-learning) available that allow individuals to complete a course of study while working full time. However, be careful what you wish for. The online education industry has become a jungle of questionable for-profit education and training programs. Start with exploring www.ed2go.com and then check out cautionary tales in signing up for such programs by searching "online education caution scams." Many distance-learning programs have a reputation for engaging in fraud – set up to tap into the lucrative federal tuition assistance pipeline but produce little in terms of quality education and training. Indeed, many programs have graduation rates of less than 10 percent, and few of their graduates find employment related to their education.

If you don't have the "necessary" degree, but have a lot of work-related experience – especially if you have held the same or very similar job in the past – put together an "achievement" folder or portfolio. Build a case (with documentation) demonstrating what things you have done that "qualify" you for this position. For example, if you presently hold a job, or have held a job in the past, where you successfully performed the activities that would be required in the position you want to apply for, that is helpful. Specify each of the activities one by one, and demonstrate by examples you can talk about and, if possible, letters of recommendation you can show the employer about the specific things you did that qualify you to be considered for the job.

It is critical that you be able to talk specifically about your achievements in the job, and your case will be strengthened if you can give references that will support your assertions of the work you did. The more you can specifically **document**, the better.

BARRIER #2
Lack sufficient work experience

QUESTIONS: Do you lack sufficient work experience for the position you are going after? Do you need to find ways to convince employers that you can do the job despite your lack of experience?

IF YES: You don't have to be a rocket scientist to understand why an employer would prefer to hire someone who has prior experience successfully completing the tasks that will be required of the person hired for the job. If, you've done the job successfully before, that is a good indication you can do the work, and the added bonus is that the employer won't have to spend as much time and money to train you as he/she would a newcomer to the job.

TIPS: If you have held what was essentially the same job elsewhere, you've got a head start on applicants who don't have the experience. But having experience, in itself, is not enough. You need to demonstrate to the employer that you were **good** in that job! What **proof** do you have that you can do the job? Think back to the major things you did in that job, and ask yourself what you accomplished especially well. Make a list of your major **accomplishments** – those things you did especially well. Now, can you quantify what you did? Or can you give an **example**, by means of a short one- or two-minute **story**, of what you did or how you did it?

In other words, you need to do more than merely say, *"I had a job like the one you are trying to fill, and I did it well. So hire me."* Employers are tired of hearing job applicants tell them they can do everything in order to get the job, and then once they have been hired the employer finds out they can't do the job or don't do it well. Most employers are justifiably suspicious. So try to identify the aspects of the job that you excelled at, and then find ways – before you get to the interview – to convince the employer that you aren't conning him. You really did do all those great things for your previous employer.

If you have any certificates of merit you received for your outstanding work, so much the better. Mention it. If the previous employer will give you a good recommendation, mention that and urge the interviewer to call the person. Yes, you may be filling out that employer's name on an application, but if you know you will get a great recommendation, why not stress this fact during the job interview? That will make a bigger impression.

If your previous work experience was in a different position, but one that utilized many of the same skills that will be required in the position you are applying for, your job is to make the connection clearly for the interviewer. List as many of these similar skills as you can as you prepare for the interview. Once in the interview, talk about these skills – again using examples of the similarities between the skills you used in the job you did for your previous employer and the skills required for the job you are applying for. Of course, to do this successfully requires that you understand the skills needed for the new job you hope to get.

BARRIER #3
Lack basic reading, writing, math, and digital skills

QUESTIONS: Do you lack the literacy skills necessary to do the job you seek? Do you have difficulty reading and understanding instructions that might be necessary on the job? Do you have problems writing instructions or giving directions that you may need to convey to others? And what about your capabilities to use desktop computers, laptops, tablets, and smartphones?

IF YES: Lack of literacy skills is a widespread problem. An estimated 36 million adults, or about 11% of the U.S. population (15% of the adult population) are functionally illiterate, reading at or below a third grade level. Lacking basic reading, writing, math, and computer skills, they have difficulty finding jobs, supporting families, and staying healthy. One of seven adults is unable to comprehend a job application or read the front page of a newspaper. The jobs that require the ability to read and understand fairly technical material grow yearly. Many jobs that once depended on physical strength are increasingly requiring greater mental strength as many of the heavy, repetitive, or dangerous tasks are being driven by computers and robots. So the laborer who once would have taken hand tools to rout a space in a piece of hardwood must now be able to program a computer to do the job. This takes more advanced reading and perhaps writing and mathematical skills than the job would have required a decade ago, let alone a generation ago!

Writing skills? Math skills? Same thing. Employees today may need to communicate instructions to others. Whether handwritten or using a word processing program, the ability to generate written material that is accurate and clear is an expected/required skill. Of course, the level of reading, writing, and math skills necessary varies with the job.

Digital skills are becoming increasingly important in today's workplace. How savvy are you in using a computer, sending email, texting, and understanding the latest apps? If your digital skills are weak, take an inventory of what you need to learn to improve your digital literacy. After all, employers want to hire individuals who can quickly get up to speed on the latest technology.

TIPS: Don't put off getting such education and training any longer. You simply must acquire basic literacy skills, including English-language competence. The jobs that don't require these skills become fewer each year. Start by calling your local high school or your public library and ask about the adult literacy classes offered in your community. Many communities sponsor literacy centers. For example, in New York City, contact the Literacy Assistance Center (www.lacnyc.org – Tel. 212-803-3300). The National Center for Literacy Education (www.ncte.org/ncle) includes many useful literacy resources. ProLiteracy (www.proliteracy.org) focuses on improving adult literacy in both the U.S. and worldwide.

BARRIER #4
Use poor grammar

QUESTIONS: Do you have problems speaking and writing "correct" grammar? Has your grammar suffered because of your shorthand Internet messaging and texting behavior? Do you want to improve your communication skills so you sound more educated and credible?

IF YES: Before you answer, you may want to pose this question to a few people whose expertise on this you respect and whom you trust to give you honest feedback.

If you text and email a great deal, chances are your grammar skills are less than stellar. Quick messaging encourages poor sentence structure, misspellings, and other violations of good grammar rules. For example, do you know the rules of good sentence structure, parts of speech, sentence complements, verbs, pronouns, agreement, modifiers, parallel structure, punctuation, spelling, and capitalization? All of these language elements relate to good grammar.

Often people who have problems with grammar don't realize they are making errors as they speak or write. You may think you speak correctly, and you may be right about that. On the other hand, you may speak the way your friends do, so it seems fine to you, but in reality it may not be appropriate grammar for landing the job you want or being promoted from the job you have. Thus, getting honest feedback from people you are certain do know correct grammar may be necessary.

You may ask, *"Why should this matter to the employer? If people understand what I say, why does it matter whether I use correct grammar on the job?"*

The importance of using good grammar does vary with the job. For some jobs it may not be very important. Especially if there is little interaction with clients, some employers may not view poor grammar as a problem. But if you will deal with clients or have interaction with management, poor grammar can kill your chances of getting hired or keep you from a promotion. You probably don't notice your poor grammar. If you were aware of it and knew how to easily improve it, you would speak differently. This is the reason it's recommended that you seek the opinion of others on this one – not your close friends if they speak as you do, but people whom you believe use and recognize good grammar.

The bottom line is this: the grammar you use when you speak and write affects your **credibility**. People who use good grammar are quick to recognize when someone else does not. They hear poor grammar and usually assume the person who is speaking doesn't have as much knowledge or expertise as they would think he had if he were speaking correctly. Worst of all, a person exhibiting poor grammar appears uneducated. So his credibility (the way people perceive his expertise) can suffer, and furthermore the credibility of the company he works for can be questioned as well.

TIPS: If you have any doubts about the grammar you use, contact your local high school or community college and ask about any refresher courses in grammar they may offer. Check online as well. There are a lot of basic grammar courses offered through distance-learning. Almost any online education institute or two-year college will offer refresher grammar classes. For starters, view a few popular grammar videos on YouTube, which give examples of both bad and good grammar. Also, your library may have copies of the following useful grammar books and DVDs: *501 Grammar and Writing Questions*, *Better Grammar in 30 Minutes a Day*, *The Grammar Bible*, *Grammar Success in 20 Minutes a Day*, *English Grammar Series* (DVDs), *Great Grammar Series* (DVDs), and *Upgrade Your Writing Series* (DVDs).

BARRIER #5
Use inappropriate language for the workplace

QUESTIONS: Do you frequently use words that would have to be "bleeped" from television broadcasts – swear words or sexually connotative language? Do you sometimes embarrass others with what you say? Do you have a habit of trying to impress others with your bad or raunchy language?

IF YES: If you use this kind of language, you probably use these words out of habit, and much of the time you are not even aware you are using them. These words may have become a part of your day-to-day speech. Swearing or sexual innuendo do not belong in any workplace. However, swearing may likely be overlooked on a large construction site for a commercial building, but less likely to be tolerated on a remodeling or expansion of a client's home. Swearing at or around clients is unacceptable and is generally not tolerated in an office setting. Sexual innuendo cannot be tolerated by employers because allowing it in the workplace is against the law. No employer wants to be hit with a sexual harassment lawsuit.

If you are in the habit of using inappropriate language, the sooner you "clean up your act" the better. If you engage in such language only occasionally, you can probably deal with this on your own by recognizing it as a potential barrier and resolving to modify your actions. However, if you insert inappropriate language liberally into your conversations, it is a habit that will take some attention and time to break.

TIPS: Enlist the aid of a trusted friend to help you become aware each time you make a comment that would not be appropriate in the workplace you aspire to. As time passes, you will become more aware of these yourself – although probably **after** you have made the remark. As more time passes and you gain awareness of these inappropriate remarks, you will reach a point when you are aware you are about to make the remark. It is at this point that you can **change** your behavior by modifying the remark to something more appropriate – or saying nothing at all. Silence is a lot better than having one's foot in one's mouth!

BARRIER #6
Lack workplace skills

QUESTIONS: Do you lack basic workplace skills expected for the job you want? Do you need to acquire more skills?

IF YES: Workplace skills vary widely with the type of job you do. For some jobs, answering the phone in a pleasant manner, taking accurate messages, and forwarding them to the right person would be considered a basic workplace skill. These days, however, for a great many jobs the basic skills require familiarity with technology. If people applying for the job you want are expected to have word processing skills, be able to use a spreadsheet, or be proficient with particular software and apps, then these are skills you must develop.

Employers expect to train new hires on equipment that is unique to their workplace or on procedures that have been put in place "in-house," but employers expect job applicants to have familiarity with equipment common to most workplaces or equipment generally required for the position that is open.

TIPS: If there are basic workplace skills you lack, then start to acquire them as soon as possible. Check with your public library, your community's adult education program, or community college as to the offerings available. Also, check online for skills training programs.

BARRIER #7
Lack a work record – have never had a job

QUESTION: Do you lack an apparent work history? Do you need to acquire some experiences that would qualify as work experience?

IF YES: You believe you have never had a job, and hence have no work record? Are you sure about that? Many people believe they have never had a job because they only worked a few hours a week, or perhaps they did volunteer work and never got paid for the work they did. Most people have some work experience. Did you mow lawns or shovel snow for people in your neighborhood as a youth? Did you get paid to babysit for a neighbor's children? Did you work as an unpaid volunteer?

TIPS: Chances are, if you search your mind hard enough, you will find that you do have some work experience. The first thing to do is make a list of anything you can think of that you have done which might qualify – put it down on paper – no matter how insignificant you think it is. Then go back over your list and ask yourself what skills you used or what level of responsibility you demonstrated as you did these jobs. When you shoveled snow, did your clients (neighbors who hired you) give you repeat business because they could depend on you to show up when you said you would and compliment you on doing the job well? Dependability and attention to detail are two of the traits most sought in a job applicant. Did the supervisor at the retirement center where you volunteered for a few hours each week during your senior year tell you how well you interacted with the residents? Good interpersonal skills are also highly valued by employers. Take a hard look at any jobs you have done, and you may find you can turn even limited experience into a positive work history.

If you truly have nothing you can cite as work experience, is there an organization whose work is consistent with your values where you might begin to work a few hours a week as a volunteer? Most charitable organizations are always in need of volunteers. You could probably start tomorrow or next week gaining work experience. Be dependable and do a good job and you'll have references for your future. If you are a student, consider an internship – whether paid or unpaid – related to the work you may want to do in the future. Not only can an internship give you valuable work experience, but often internships turn into job offers.

BARRIER #8
Lack a positive (good) work report – been fired

QUESTIONS: Have you ever been fired from a job? Have you ever been let go or laid off while others stayed behind?

IF YES: If you have been fired, let's be honest. For many employers, this is a **blazing** red flag. It is like waving a red flag in front of a bull. Most employers believe that a job applicant who has been fired is likely to mean trouble for a future employer. So it's easier to pass over the applicant with a firing in his background than to take a chance on encountering problems later. This can be a real barrier; it is not insurmountable, but it is a potential barrier if not handled properly.

On the other hand, many people get fired all the time. What's important to employers is the **reason** for your dismissal. For example, being fired for stealing, drug use, insubordination, or incompetence are very different from being fired because of changes in key personnel, personality conflicts, power struggles, mergers, or the loss of a major client account. More people are fired each year for being on the losing end of organizational politics than for incompetence. In fact, the person reviewing your credentials may have been fired more than once in his or her career!

TIPS: So what do you do? First, **be honest, but not stupid.** This means that if you are asked, on an application or in an interview, whether you have ever been fired, you tell the truth. But don't stupidly volunteer this information on anything the employer will see before he meets with you in person. If you do, the employer may prematurely judge you, and you may never have the opportunity to meet her in person (an interview) to convince her that you are right for the job.

You want to have the opportunity to meet with the employer, usually in an interview, and "sell" the employer on your qualifications for the job and calm her fears that your having been fired means that you will be a problem employee. Why were you fired? Your goal is to present the incident in the most positive, yet honest, way that you can.

Second, **take responsibility** for whatever mistakes you made or the situation you were in. Don't be judgmental or show any lingering anger. Just reveal the facts. It is so easy to lay the blame on someone else. But employers have heard all the excuses before, and you will sound like one more person who can't own up to his own mistakes. After all, if you won't take responsibility for your actions, there is little likelihood that your actions will change. It is expected that you will continue to repeat the past behavior. So ask yourself why this behavior occurred, and determine what things you have done to change the situation. For example, if you were continually absent from or late to work, why? If you were a full-time student and working two jobs and thus you frequently overslept and missed or were late to work, these reasons do not excuse your behavior. However, if your situation has changed, you are no longer taking classes or working another job, then you may be able to explain the changes in your situation well enough to convince an employer to give you a chance.

But you must indicate to the employer what you have done to change your behavior(s) so that the action(s) that led to your being fired won't occur again – on a new employer's watch. The more specific you can be about the changes you have made, the more believable your story will be. If you have several examples of steps you have taken, talk about the strongest ones.

BARRIER #9
Lack a positive (good) work record –
poor recommendation from former employer(s)

QUESTIONS: Is there a former employer(s) who is likely to give you a poor recommendation? Do you have some red flags in your work history that might surface if someone does a thorough background check?

IF YES: Most employers do background checks, which include asking for feedback from applicants' former employers. A good recommendation from a former employer offers reassurance that the job applicant can and will perform well. If you have prior work experience, but do not receive good recommendations, this unfurls another red flag to a potential future employer. This is another serious barrier. Let's see how you can get around it.

TIPS: The first and most obvious question you should ask yourself is, why? Why are you unable to get a good recommendation from this employer? Once you identify the problem(s), the rest of the steps are similar to those suggested above for someone who has been fired.

1. Identify the problem behavior.
2. Take responsibility for your actions.
3. Determine what caused the behavior(s) to occur.
4. What steps have you taken to change the situation so the problem behavior will not be repeated?

In the job interview, be ready to talk honestly, but as positively about these things as you can. You need to have thought this out thoroughly prior to the interview. Don't try to memorize anything, but be prepared with the gist of what you want to convey to the prospective employer. Be specific and support your assertions with examples.

BARRIER #10
Lack a positive (good) work record – have been a "job hopper"

QUESTIONS: Have you changed jobs more than once in the past two years? More than twice in the past three years? Do you have difficulty keeping motivated and focused on a job? Are you unclear what you want to do? Are you a serial job hopper employers wish to avoid hiring?

IF YES: Advertising a vacant position and going through the hiring process is costly for employers. Add to that the cost of training a new hire, and you can understand that replacing an employee adds expenses that cut into company profits. Every employer wants to hire good workers who will stay with the company for more than a few weeks or months. If your resume shows that you have a pattern of changing jobs frequently, that is likely to be a barrier. The employer would rather hire a good worker who will stay around for a while.

TIPS: Look at the tips above directed at the person without a good recommendation. Several of these tips should work well in your situation too. Identify the reason(s) you keep changing jobs.

What is different about this job you are applying for? If you are hired, why do you expect to keep this job longer than the ones in the past? If you can be convincing with regard to these two questions looming in the employer's mind, this should not disqualify you unless you have been a job hopper to the extreme.

BARRIER #11
Have more education, training, and/or experience than the position requires

QUESTIONS: Are you overqualified for the position you will apply for? Do you want to find a job that is more compatible with your qualifications? Do you need to refocus your resume?

IF YES: You may think being overqualified for a position should work in your favor, but that is not usually the case. Being a little bit overqualified might be a plus, but if your qualifications are well beyond what is required for the job, that is going to work against you. Why, you may ask, would an employer not feel fortunate to be able to hire someone overqualified to fill a position?

The short answer is this: the employer thinks that those who accept a job well beneath their qualifications will not stay in the job very long. The assumption is that you are taking the job, because you need a job right now, and as soon you get a better offer, you will quit. Then the employer will have to go through the process of filling the position again – a costly process.

TIPS: First, level with yourself. Why do you want this job? Are you settling for something less than you are qualified for and would really like to do? If so, refocus your efforts on a more appropriate goal.

If you really do want this job, even though your training, education, or/and experience would qualify you for a higher level position, know that you are going to have to convince a skeptical employer. So begin by listing the reasons you want this position. For each reason, ask yourself how you might support it to make it convincing to an employer. Then be ready to talk about this with great conviction in the interview. If the employer doesn't bring up the matter of your apparent over-qualifications, **you must** do so. Because whether she mentions it or not, this will be an potential knock-out factor in the mind of the employer. You must make or seize the opportunity to convince the interviewer of your sincerity in wanting **this** position, and your commitment to the job and staying with the job for a reasonable period of time.

BARRIER #12
Lack technology skills (not technologically savvy)

QUESTION: Do you lack basic computer and digital skills? Do you wish you knew how to better use email, apps, and the Internet? Would many employers not hire you because you're unfamiliar with many computer programs and related technology? Are you a slow keyboarder?

IF YES: You are probably aware that information technology (IT) impacts our lives from the workplace to our homes. Although there are some jobs for which IT skills are not necessary, more and more jobs require at least basic IT skills. Even in the auto industry, traditionally an occupation where good money could be made without a lot of education or prior training, computer technology has made many jobs obsolete and increased the technological skills necessary to do other jobs.

Although most employers will train a new hire in computer skills specific to the industry or the job, employers expect job candidates today to bring basic computer skills to the workplace.

TIPS: Training in IT is widely available and basic skills can be learned with a minimum investment of time and money. If you need basic skills training, check with your local library, and ask if they offer any training or if they can refer you to courses available in your area. Most community colleges will offer these classes, or check with your community's American Job Center (jobcenter.usa.gov). There are a lot of courses available online as well, if you have a skill level that allows you to search online and register for a course. Visit any website offering certificate programs or two-year degrees and you will find many IT offerings. Or use a search engine, such as Google, to search for the type of course you need.

If you are applying for a computer technology job, of course you will need skills beyond the basic level. Check your library, community college, Americam Job Center, or go online and register for classes to expand your IT skills.

4

Attitudes and Behaviors as Barriers

"Red flags relating to specific behaviors can be quickly corrected once you acknowledge the problems and take actions to modify them. If you don't, they may turn into intractable bad habits that can plague you the rest of your life!"

T HE RED FLAGS ADDRESSED in Chapter 3 require more time to change than red flags in this and subsequent chapters, because they deal with **long-term preparation** for life and the workplace. For example, if you need additional education or training to qualify for the job you want, you must take some time (3 to 48 months) to acquire the necessary skills.

Behavioral changes often take time, too – although some take more time than others. A **habit** is a behavior that you have engaged in for a long period of time and may not be easily modified, whereas other behaviors might be changed in a matter of days if you are committed to making the change.

BARRIER #13
Engage in self-destructive behaviors – drug abuse

QUESTIONS: Do you use illegal drugs? Do you abuse over-the-counter or prescription drugs? Do you think you may have a problem passing an employment drug screening test? Are you in denial?

IF YES: This is an "either you do or you don't" question. You either use illegal drugs or you don't. If you are hesitant or "iffy" as to how to respond, the honest answer is probably "yes." But why should this pose an employment problem?

First, it is by definition an illegal activity. If you are caught, there is much more than your job at stake. Beyond that, which you may say is your risk and your business, why should an employer care? Aside from what you may wish to believe in an attempt to rationalize your behavior, few people who use illegal drugs are able to do so for very long before it begins to affect their performance at work. Absences from work tend to become more frequent. Concentration is less focused and, over time, work suffers. Driving may become impaired. Second, more and more employers have a zero tolerance policy regarding illegal drug use. They require drug testing as part of the hiring process as well as subject employees to random drug testing. If you don't pass the drug test, you won't get the job or you will probably be fired. Ask yourself this: Is your drug habit really worth losing a job?

An employer takes a risk every time he hires a new employee. If a new hire uses illegal drugs, that risk is greatly increased.

TIPS: The obvious suggestion is, don't use illegal drugs. If you use them only occasionally and can stop any time (as many people claim), then stop **now** – while you can. If you are addicted, seek out a drug rehabilitation or substance abuse program and commit yourself to getting yourself drug-free. Several websites can assist you in locating the right program:

- www.samhsa.gov
- www.drug-rehabs.com
- www.soberrecovery.com
- www.hazelden.org

Several books, which can be found through the publisher's online bookstore (www.impactpublications.com), can assist you with addiction and recovery issues:

- *A to Z of Addictions and Addictive Behaviors*
- *The Addiction Workbook*
- *The Addictive Personality*
- *Addictive Thinking*
- *Breaking Addiction*
- *Denial Is Not a River in Egypt*

- *Ending Addiction for Good*
- *How to Quit Drugs for Good!*
- *The Recovery Book*
- *Sex, Drugs, Gambling, and Chocolate*
- *Stop the Chaos!*

BARRIER #14
Engage in self-destructive behaviors – alcohol abuse

QUESTIONS: Do you ever drink alcohol during the day, such as before 5pm on work days? Do you ever feel you have to have a drink to be able to get through the day? Have you had so much to drink that you have done things that embarrassed you (or should have) – perhaps at the office holiday party? Do you hide a bottle of your favorite alcoholic beverage somewhere in your office? Are you ever not able to recall what happened the day before, or the night before?

IF YES: Whether you want to admit it or not, chances are you have a problem if you answered "yes" to any of those questions. The chances increase if, after an honest reflection and soul searching, you answered "yes" to more than one question above.

An employee's alcohol consumption only becomes of concern to, or the business of, the employer when the alcohol interferes with the employee's job performance. However, most people who drink too much, even to the point of actually being alcoholics, don't believe they have a problem. They will deny, even to the point of hiding empty bottles, the reality of their alcohol problem, and refuse to admit their problem to themselves. It is this **denial** that makes this barrier an especially difficult one to address. After all, one has to admit he or she has a problem before any progress can be made in overcoming it.

TIPS: First, be honest with yourself. Don't continue to deny you have a problem until you "hit bottom" and are finally forced to accept it. The sooner you accept and face your problem, the sooner you can begin overcoming this particular barrier and start on your way to a better employment picture. The advantage you have is that there are lots of resources available to help people who are addicted to alcohol. Most communities have a chapter of Alcoholics Anonymous which you should consider joining: www.aa.org. A good starting point for locating a substance abuse program nearest you is the federal government's gateway site to treatment centers:

www.samhsa.gov

The following self-directed books, which also are available through Impact Publications, can help in overcoming alcohol-related addictions:

- *Alcoholics Anonymous: Big Book*
- *Alcoholism and Addiction Cure*
- *A Gentle Path Through the Twelve Steps*
- *How to Get Sober and Stay Sober*
- *Sober But Stuck*

BARRIER #15
Engage in self-destructive behaviors – excessive gambling

QUESTIONS: Do you gamble a great deal? Are you a compulsive gambler? Do your gambling losses sometimes put you at financial risk? Does gambling affect your work and your relationships with others?

IF YES: If you do gamble, be honest with yourself in answering these questions. Like drug and alcohol abuse, gambling often becomes an **addiction** that is difficult to overcome on your own. It has both personal and professional consequences which many people are quick to deny.

TIPS: Changing behavior is much more difficult than you may think. People in denial first refuse to admit they have a problem. Once they recognize they have a problem, they next believe they can deal with the issue on their own. They feel they are strong enough to just say "no" and go on with their lives. However, in reality few people can break addictions by going "cold turkey" on their own. They need **professional help** and some type of **support system** to help them change the way they make decisions. One of the first places to start is by joining a 12-step self-help Gamblers Anonymous program, which may operate in or near your community. They usually have meeting space at a church or hospital and meet once a week to talk through their situations and share their insights into their addiction. You can find a group nearest your home by exploring this website: www.gamblersanonymous.org.

BARRIER #16
Steal from employer or others

QUESTIONS: Have you ever stolen anything of greater value than a paperclip or a pencil? Do you sometimes come to work late and leave early? Do you often use the Internet and telephone at work for personal business?

IF YES: You can understand an employer's reluctance to hire someone who has a record of stealing. Obvious reasons for a prospective employer's concern include whether you will steal from your next employer – him. If you have contact with clients, especially in their homes, will you steal from them, thereby putting the company at risk of a lawsuit or/and bad publicity?

Know too, that you don't just steal from your employer by pilfering goods or supplies. Stealing involves appropriating time and services from your employer. Indeed, the most common workplace theft is **time**. If you spend time at work on the Internet or telephone doing personal things such as shopping online or chatting and texting with friends, if you take longer than authorized breaks or lunch time, if you add time you didn't really work to your time card, make personal copies on the copy machine or use the postage meter for personal mail without asking permission, you are guilty of theft! How then do you handle this issue in an interview?

TIPS: If you have committed a theft in the past, were you caught? If you weren't caught, it happened a long time ago, you have not repeated the offense, and you honestly don't think it will ever happen again, there is no reason to bring it up in your job interview – assuming you are not applying for a job where you will be expected to pass a polygraph test as a condition of employment. In other words, be honest but not stupid. The interview is not a confessional.

If you were caught, prosecuted, and found guilty, then you probably have a record or rap sheet. If you stole from your employer and were caught, you may not have been prosecuted, but you certainly don't expect to get a glowing job reference. So how do you handle this? First, do not put this on your resume, and try to avoid putting this information on a job application. You want an interview with the employer and the chance to convince him that you know you made a mistake in the past, you take responsibility for your actions, and that you have made changes in your situation so that the "red flag" behavior will not be repeated.

If you have a history of petty theft (you believe no one will really notice) or stealing time by doing personal business during company hours or coming to work late or leaving early, you are still a thief. Although you may not think so, time stealers are usually easy to detect. Co-workers know who is doing what and when, and bosses keep an eye on employees who are less than attentive to their work. More and more employers also are monitoring the Internet time of their employees by installing software for tracking Internet use. Once you lose the trust of your employer because of such time thefts, your job and future with the employer will never be the same. **Trust** is one of the most important ingredients in any relationship. Once you become untrustworthy, it's just a matter of time before you lose your job. Your goal should be to become a highly valued and trusted employee who **exceeds expectations** of employers.

BARRIER #17
Make excuses rather than take responsibility

QUESTIONS: Do you make excuses for bad behavior rather than accept responsibility? Is it always someone else who creates a problem or gets you into trouble? Do you usually come up with excuses for not doing things you should be doing?

IF YES: Sometimes it seems easier to place the blame for our shortcomings on others rather than to take responsibility for our own actions. If you were fired from a previous job, it was someone else's fault. Your boss "had it in for you" or you were the "fall guy" for someone else's mistake. But most employers have heard the excuses before and are unimpressed and unconvinced. When a job candidate places the blame for his past problems on others, it says far more about the person making the excuse than about the person he is trying to blame.

Employers often encounter 25 excuses related to the workplace. Some are even used by candidates during a job interview to explain their questionable on-the-job behavior! Most of these excuses reflect an **attitude lacking in responsibility and initiative**:

1. No one told me.
2. I did what you said.
3. Your directions were bad.
4. It's not my fault.
5. She did it.
6. It just seemed to happen.
7. It happens a lot.
8. What did he say?
9. I had a headache.
10. I don't understand why.
11. I don't know how to do it.
12. That's your problem.
13. It wasn't very good.
14. Maybe you did it.
15. I thought I wrote it down.
16. That's not my style.
17. He told me to do it that way.
18. I've got to go now.
19. Where do you think it went?
20. We can talk about it later.
21. My computer crashed.
22. The Internet went down.
23. I think someone gave me a virus.
24. I didn't get your email. Where did you send it?
25. My prayers weren't answered.

We all make excuses. Many are harmless excuses that help us get through the day. Identify a few excuses you frequently make. What, for example, would you say to an interviewer if you arrived late for a job interview? What would you say if someone asks you why you dropped out of school, quit a job, or were fired from a job? Who was responsible for those actions?

When you offer excuses for your behavior, you literally show an attitude that is not appreciated by employers. Indeed, your attitude toward personal responsibility shows. People with positive attitudes and proactive behavior do not engage in behaviors that reflect such excuses. They have a "can do" attitude that focuses on the future. That attitude helps focus their minds on doing those things that are most important to achieving their goals. For example, rather than show up 10 minutes late for a job interview and say they got lost or had bad directions, people with positive attitudes and proactive behavior check out the interview location the day before in anticipation of arriving 10 minutes early. They make no excuses, because they plan ahead and engage in no-excuses behavior!

TIPS: Take **responsibility** for mistakes you have made and **learn** from those experiences. In so doing, you will make a far better impression on the interviewer than you will by pointing your finger at someone else.

Enhance your credibility by indicating that you learned something from the situation that went wrong. You know the adage, *"When life gives you lemons, make lemonade."* You can turn a negative situation into a positive one and overcome a barrier by accepting responsibility, indicating what lessons you learned from it, and what you would do differently if faced with that or a similar situation in the future. You will make a far better impression than you will by shirking responsibility and placing the blame on someone else.

BARRIER #18
Speak negatively about others

QUESTIONS: Do you "badmouth" or speak negatively about former employers and co-workers? Do you try to build yourself up at the expense of others?

IF YES: This is similar to the previous barrier, but in this instance a person just makes disparaging remarks in general about others. Some people are narcissists. Other people do this out of an inferiority complex. They try to make themselves feel more important by verbally running others down. Others tend to be very opinionated and intolerant of others. Such remarks usually say more about the person making the remarks than about the subject of the negative comments, and hence don't serve the speaker well. If you speak negatively about former employers or co-workers during a job interview, the interviewer will assume that, if hired, you will do the same about her someday. You'll also probably be a negative influence in the company, lowering morale as you talk others down in your attempt to build yourself up in the eyes of others. Such individuals are more trouble than they are worth.

TIPS: Self-assured people with positive self-esteem don't need to "run others down" to enhance their self-image. You will leave a far more favorable impression by being gracious in your remarks about others. When you speak in a positive manner about others, you indicate that you are supportive of them and enjoy working with them. Indeed, you are probably a **good team player**.

BARRIER #19
Gossip about others

QUESTIONS: Do you gossip about your boss and co-workers? Do you enjoy getting the dirt on others and telling malicious stories? Do you like to stand out from the crowd by embellishing stories about other people?

IF YES: One dictionary defines gossip as "idle talk or rumor about the personal affairs of others." Hence, gossip isn't necessarily malicious – although it can be. Why would an employer care if you gossip? First, gossiping can make you appear shallow. There's an old saying that goes like this: *"Small people talk about other people; medium people talk about things; and big people talk about ideas."* Second, gossip, whether intended as malicious or not, can hurt others. People whose feelings have been hurt may be distracted from their job or they may find it hard to work with other employees in this situation. Third, gossiping in the workplace steals time from the employer and takes other people's focus off their work. Fourth, gossip can damage morale and thus negatively affect productivity. If you get a reputation as the **company gossip**, many co-workers will be reluctant to share their personal stories with you, because they know you're likely to "spread the word" on them as well.

TIP: Don't gossip about other people in a job interview or on the job. Doing so in a job interview will lessen your chance of being hired, and once you are on the job, gossip can break your chance of promotion. Remember, gossip is talking about the personal affairs of others. So this rule does not preclude your talking about work you have done or are doing with others, or work you have done for a former employer.

BARRIER #20
Appear self-centered rather than employer-centered

QUESTIONS: Are you or do you appear self-centered? Do you talk a lot about "I" or "me" rather than "you" or "us"? Does your **objective** relate to the needs of employers or to your own needs?

IF YES: It is only human to be interested in ourselves and our own welfare. However, when interviewing with an employer whom you hope will

hire you and pay you money, common sense should suggest to an applicant that the major focus of interest should be on the job and the employer. It is a bright red flag to an employer when an applicant only seems to
be interested in the salary and fringe benefits that come with a job. At the
same time, try to focus on the needs of the employer and the requirements
of the job. Instead of talking about "I" or "me," focus on "you" or "us."

TIP: Avoid talking about benefits or salary early in the job interview. It
is to your advantage for any mention of money to be put off as long as
possible – until the employer brings it up or you are being offered the
job. As you talk with the interviewer, focus your comments on the job,
the company, and the employer. Talk about your previous work experience in terms of how it has prepared you to do the job this employer is
interviewing you for. **Give examples** of work you have done that relate
to the job under consideration. **Ask questions and listen** for the answers that tell you about the job – both what it entails (what you would
do and the skills you would use) and what the employer needs. Focus
on what you can do for the employer.

BARRIER #21
Brag about yourself

QUESTIONS: Are you a braggart? Are you a name-dropper who tries
to impress others with your so-called connections to influential people?
Do you think you're smarter than most other people you meet or associ-
ate with? Are you a classic insecure narcissist who feels he's always the
smartest person in the room and whose object of affection is his reflection?

IF YES: In the name of being self-assured, confident, and impressive,
do you brag to others about your skills, your accomplishments, your
possessions, or your connections to influential people? Certainly you
want to appear self-assured both in the job interview and on the job. But
there is a difference between appearing self-assured and being cocky,
arrogant, or insecure. People get tired of hearing others constantly brag
about themselves; they try to avoid such people as irritating bores.
These tend to be insecure individuals who turn off others with their
self-centered stories and name-dropping. Thus, an employer is reluctant
to hire someone who comes across as boastful or too cocky. An employ-

er wants to hire individuals with whom he believes he will enjoy working, and whom he believes will get along well with co-workers as well as with clients. Besides being obnoxious, a braggart often makes others suspicious that he is trying to hide some inadequacy or insecurities.

TIP: Of course, in the job interview you will want to talk about the successes you have had doing things similar to those that will be required in the new position. But focus on the job that was done, rather than how great you were for doing it. Sprinkle some "we's" as you talk, along with "I." That suggests you can work as part of a team and that you are willing to share the credit. For example, you might say the following when talking about your past accomplishments during a job interview:

> When I was at AXY, I suggested the company use a different inventory system. We implemented the new system, and within one quarter we had improved our efficiency by 50%. We cut down on overstocks and returns, as well as rush orders which required overnight delivery resulting in high shipping costs. The company saved over $500,000 in the first year after the new system was implemented.

While you've taken credit for an important productivity initiative it was your idea – you also focused on the company's savings and the team ("we") that made it happen. This is a win-win story: **you** get credit for the idea, the **team** gets credit for implementing it, and the **company** comes away with a significant savings! That's the kind of person employers want to hire and join their team. Now, if you also said the above with **enthusiasm**, you've really made a positive impression. Your goal is to appear confident, but not cocky.

BARRIER #22
Exhibit a temper and express anger

QUESTIONS: Do you have a temper that is often out of control? Have you failed to get promoted because of anger issues? Do you have a negative and pessimistic attitude toward life? Do you feel other people try to take advantage of you?

IF YES: Angry behavior is disruptive behavior in relationships as well as in the workplace. It impacts everyone within earshot, and causes them to lose focus on the work they are doing. It's abusive behavior that can cause bad feelings between workers, and hence create barriers to their working together as a team. It's a leading cause of workplace violence. Indeed, anger can escalate to the point that it becomes threatening and expressed in violent behaviors as evidenced by the number of employees (and former employees) who enter the workplace with a gun and leave supervisors and co-workers wounded or dead. A temper that is out of control is a barrier to employment and to advancement. It puts other employees at risk and creates liabilities for employers who are supposed to maintain a collegial and safe workplace. Extremely angry people often express rage – an uncontrolled form of anger that can become very violent. Approximately five percent of the population suffers from IED (Intermittent Explosive Disorder), a recently diagnosed form of impulsive anger found in some individuals that only occasionally surfaces, such as road rage.

While angry people often get their way through intimidation, they also suffer the consequences of such behavior. Angry people are often passed over for promotion and many are fired. Indeed, more people are fired because of anger issues than for incompetence. Anger is also a leading cause of stress-related health problems, especially heart disease. If you have a negative and pessimistic attitude toward life, you also may harbor many angry feelings.

TIP: Each of us becomes angry at times; that is only human. How we control and channel our anger is what's important to maintaining healthy and productive relationships. If your anger is disruptive to the workplace, it is time to admit the problem and seek help. There are many good books on controlling anger, and if you are well motivated, you may find a book or two on the subject is all you need. You might start with my *Anger Management Pocket Guide* as well as examine these titles:

- *Anger and Conflict in the Workplace*
- *Angry Men*
- *Angry Women*
- *Beyond Anger: A Guide for Men*
- *Controlling People*
- *Of Course You're Angry*
- *The Anger Workbook*

On the other hand, if your anger level is severe, you may need professional help. Seek assistance from community anger control programs. You can find information on such programs through community service organizations, family services departments, the court system, and local churches. Visit these websites for information on anger control programs and courses:

- www.angermanagement.org
- www.angermanagementonline.com
- www.courseforanger.com
- www.anger-management.com
- www.onlineangercourse.com
- www.courtorderedclasses.com
- www.anger-management-classes.net
- www.ajnovickgroup.com
- www.angercoach.com
- www.angermgmt.com

BARRIER #23
Express intolerance of others

QUESTIONS: Are you intolerant of opinions that differ from your own? Do you argue with others rather than try to see their point of view? Do you respond to controversial opinions by saying *"That's an interesting thought. Have you considered.....?"* or *"You're wrong. I can't believe you think that way!"*?

IF YES: People from differing backgrounds who might not form friendships outside the workplace are often thrown together in a work setting. How do you react when faced with someone who holds opinions that differ – perhaps greatly – from your own? What if your job requires that you work together? What happens then? Are you opinionated to the extreme? Do you feel compelled to try to convince the other person of the error of his ways? Do you tell him he is wrong? Do you call him names or tell him anyone who believes the way he does is stupid? Do you find it difficult or impossible to work with someone who holds such differing views?

Employers have the right to expect that the people who work for them can get along and are able to work together to get the job done.

As a part of the job interview, one of the things an interviewer tries to determine is how well an applicant interacts with others and is likely to work with co-workers. If you cannot work cooperatively with others, including those who have beliefs or attitudes very different from your own, it will be a barrier to getting or keeping most jobs as well as to being promoted.

TIP: Intolerant people are often their own worst enemies. They sabotage relationships for some of the silliest reasons. Most of us are drawn to people who share similar views to our own. These people's beliefs are consistent with our own and serve as validation of the choices we make. You are familiar with the adage, *"Birds of a feather flock together."* Although it is natural to form bonds with those who share our views, a person with a mature and healthy sense of self-identity does not feel threatened by people just because they hold a different viewpoint. The valued employee is one who gets along well with all the other workers, superiors, and subordinates. Try to avoid being confrontational and contentious with others. Most people do not respond well to aggressive and disagreeable people. They become defensive and argumentative. Rather than confront others with differing ideas or opinions by being disagreeable, respond by making a neutral observation and raising questions: *"That's an interesting idea. Do many others share your feelings? What do you think would happen if.....?"* You may wish to avoid controversial subjects. Try to draw the person out rather than confront them in what will inevitably become a negative confrontation with hard feelings expressed by both parties. Try to separate the individual from his ideas. You can still get along with people, even like them, despite some of their stupid ideas! Indeed, some of your best and most interesting friends might be ones who do not share your ideas. You get along with them because you enjoy being around them.

BARRIER #24
Lack initiative and self-motivation

QUESTIONS: Do you lack initiative and self-motivation? Do you wait to be told what to do at work? When you finish your assigned work, do you piddle until you are given something else to do?

IF YES: If you lack self-motivation to show up for work regularly and on time, or if you require constant supervision to keep you from slacking off, this is a huge barrier to successful employment – both getting and keeping a job. Most employers don't want to constantly supervise or micro-manage their workers. Employers prefer to hire people who are self-starters, individuals who, once they understand the job to be done, can be counted on to carry through and complete the task to the best of their ability and the employer's expectations.

TIPS: Individuals who lack motivation and initiative are likely to stay near the bottom of the employment ladder. No one wants to hire a warm body that sits around waiting to be told what to do. If you lack motivation to become a productive employee, chances are you have an attitude problem and you lack goals. You also may have low self-esteem and find yourself in the wrong job. The following books will help you change your attitude as well as your motivation:

- *7 Habits of Highly Effective People*
- *100 Ways to Motivate Yourself*
- *Attitude Is Everything*
- *Awaken the Giant Within*
- *Change Your Attitude*
- *Change Your Thinking, Change Your Life*
- *Goals!*
- *Maximum Achievement*
- *The Power of Positive Thinking*
- *Reinventing Yourself*
- *The Success Principles*

If taking initiative is an issue with you, begin thinking about how you can better approach your job. Develop a list of your ongoing duties and responsibilities as well as identify your major accomplishments during the past month. Identify what new responsibilities you have taken on by yourself. Develop a list of additional things you could do to improve the operations of your organization. How, for example, could you solve a problem, make more money, or save money for your employer? What ideas do you have that would contribute to improving the bottom line of the company? Develop a plan that would enable you to contribute more to the company. Read the following books:

- *12 Bad Habits That Hold Good People Back*
- *How to Be a Star At Work*
- *The One Thing You Need to Know*
- *Overcoming 101 More Employment Barriers*
- *What Your Boss Doesn't Tell You Until It's Too Late*

If your lack of motivation relates to your current job and the nature of your work, you should consider changing jobs and careers. In fact, many people are unhappy with their jobs because they are in the wrong jobs. Find out what you really do well and enjoy doing by conducting a through self-assessment (see my companion assessment book, ***I Want to Do Something Else, But I'm Not Sure What It Is***). Once you've identified what really turns you on in the workplace – motivates you to excel and love your work – begin looking for a job that is the perfect fit for your motivated abilities and skills.

BARRIER #25
Lack dependability and trustworthiness

QUESTIONS: Do you lack dependability and trustworthiness? Do you sometimes come to work late and fail to complete your assignments in a timely manner? Do you ever lie to or try to deceive your employer?

IF YES: Trust is the glue that keeps relationships and organizations together. If someone can't trust you, they will try to keep you at arm's length and avoid entrusting you with important matters. Why should they invest more time and money in someone who is potentially more trouble than they are worth? Employers are not stupid. They know who is and is not dependable and trustworthy. They quickly learn who is truthful and who is deceptive. Once you are suspected of lying or deception, you lose all credibility. You will be shut out of choice assignments, raises, and promotions. You will become a dead-end employee whose future with the organization will be in question. Once you cannot be trusted, whatever positive relationship you had with your employer will never be the same. You'll soon be shown the door.

TIPS: You basically have two approaches to overcoming this barrier. Remember, you are trying to repair what may be an irreparably damaged relationship. First, quickly change your behavior by becoming dependable, truthful, and trustworthy at all times. This may mean meeting with your boss to discuss your problem and what you have done to change your behavior. The second option is to find another job where you can make a fresh start by becoming very dependable and trustworthy. As you may quickly discover, good things tend to happen to dependable and trustworthy employees!

BARRIER #26
Exhibit negative attitudes and character

QUESTIONS: Do you hang around depressing people who use lots of negative terms such as "can't," "won't," and "shouldn't"? Do you often talk yourself out of doing things, because you believe something negative will happen as a consequence? Is your glass usually half empty rather than half full? Do you express negative thoughts to others who may find that you are a depressing person to hang around? Do you avoid doing certain things because you are afraid of rejections? Are you sometimes envious of people who seem to have a positive outlook on life and who appear to be very successful?

IF YES: People with negative attitudes tend to attract negative outcomes. Take, for example, the job search, which is all about making good first impressions on strangers who know little or nothing about your background and capabilities. Whether completing an application, writing a resume, or interviewing for a job, you will reveal your attitude in many different ways, both verbally and nonverbally.

Many job seekers show attitudes of disrespect, deceit, laziness, irresponsibility, and carelessness – all red flags that will quickly knock you out of the competition. Most of these attitudes are communicated during the critical job interview when employers have a chance to read both verbal and nonverbal behavioral cues. Here are some common mistakes job seekers make that show off some killer attitudes that also reflect on their character:

Mistake	Attitude/Character
■ Lacks a job objective	Confused and unfocused
■ Misspells words on resume, application, and/or letter	Careless and inconsiderate
■ Uses poor grammar	Uneducated
■ Sends resume to wrong person	Careless and error-prone

▪ Arrives late for job interview	Unreliable
▪ Dresses inappropriately	Unperceptive and insensitive
▪ Knows little about company	Lazy and thoughtless
▪ Talks about salary and benefits	Greedy and self-centered
▪ Badmouths former employer	Disrespectful and angry
▪ Doesn't admit to weaknesses	Disingenuous and calculating
▪ Boasts about himself	Obnoxious and self-centered
▪ Lies about background	Deceitful
▪ Lacks eye contact	Shifty and dishonest
▪ Blames others for problems	Irresponsible
▪ Interrupts and argues	Inconsiderate and inflexible
▪ Has trouble answering questions	Unprepared and nervous
▪ Fails to ask any questions	Uninterested in job
▪ Jumps from one extreme to another	Manic and disorganized
▪ Fails to close and follow up interview	Doesn't care about the job

On the other hand, employers look for attitudes that indicate a candidate has some of the following positive characteristics:

▪ Accurate	▪ Fair	▪ Purposeful
▪ Adaptable	▪ Focused	▪ Reliable
▪ Careful	▪ Good-natured	▪ Resourceful
▪ Competent	▪ Happy	▪ Respectful
▪ Considerate	▪ Helpful	▪ Responsible
▪ Cooperative	▪ Honest	▪ Self-motivated
▪ Dependable	▪ Intelligent	▪ Sensitive
▪ Determined	▪ Loyal	▪ Sincere
▪ Diligent	▪ Nice	▪ Skilled
▪ Discreet	▪ Open-minded	▪ Tactful
▪ Educated	▪ Patient	▪ Team player
▪ Efficient	▪ Perceptive	▪ Tenacious
▪ Empathic	▪ Precise	▪ Tolerant
▪ Energetic	▪ Predictable	▪ Trustworthy
▪ Enthusiastic	▪ Prompt	▪ Warm

TIPS: If you have negative attitudes, you are probably an unhappy person. It's time you took control of both your attitudes and behaviors. Start by identifying several of your negative attitudes and try to transform them into positive attitudes. As you do this, you will begin to identify the positive attitude (person) you want to be. For starters, examine these sets of negative and positive attitudes that can arise at various stages of the job search, especially during the critical job interview:

- Negative Attitude	+ Positive Attitude
- I didn't like my last employer.	+ It was time for me to move on to a more progressive company.
- I haven't been able to find a job in over three months. I really want this one.	+ I've been learning a great deal during the past several weeks of my job search.
- My last two jobs were problems.	+ I learned a great deal about what I really love to do from those last two jobs.
- Do you have a job for me?	+ I'm in the process of conducting a job search. Do you know anyone who might have an interest in someone with my qualifications?
- I can't come in for an interview tomorrow since I'm interviewing for another job. What about Wednesday? That looks good.	+ I have a conflict tomorrow. Wednesday would be good. Could we do something in the morning?
- Yes, I flunked out of college in my sophomore year.`	+ After two years in college I decided to pursue a career in computer sales.
- I really hated studying math.	+ Does this job require math?
- Sorry about that spelling error on my resume. I was never good at spelling.	+ (Doesn't point it out; if asked, said *"It's one that got away."*)
- I don't enjoy working in teams.	+ I work best when given an assignment that allows me to work on my own.
- What does this job pay?	+ How does the pay scale here compare with other firms in the area?
- Will I have to work weekends?	+ What are the normal hours for someone in this position?
- I have to see my parole officer once a month. Can I have that day off?	+ I have an appointment I need to keep the last Friday of each month. Would it be okay if I took off three hours that day?

- I'm three months pregnant. your health care program cover my delivery?

- I've just got out of prison and need a job.

+ Could you tell me more about Will your benefits, such as health and dental care?

+ While incarcerated, I turned my life around by getting my GED, learning new skills, and controlling my anger. I'm really excited about becoming a landscape architect and working with your company.

Can you think of any particular negative attitudes you might have that you can restate in positive language? Identify five that relate to your job search and work. State them in both the negative and positive:

- Negative Attitude	**+ Positive Attitude**
1.	
2.	
3.	
4.	
5.	

You'll find numerous books, audiobooks, videos, and software specializing in developing positive thinking. Most are designed to transform the thinking and perceptions of individuals by changing negative attitudes. One of the major themes underlying these products is that you can change your life through positive thinking. Individuals whose lives are troubled, for example, can literally transform themselves by changing their thinking in new and positive directions. These products are especially popular with people in sales careers who must constantly stay motivated and positive in the face of making cold calls that result in numerous rejections. Positive thinking helps them get through the day, the week, and the month despite numerous rejections that would normally dissuade most people from continuing to pursue more sales calls that result in even more rejections.

One of the most important books on self-transformation through positive thinking is Napoleon Hill's *Think and Grow Rich*. This single book has had a tremendous influence on the development of the positive thinking industry, which now includes hundreds of motivational speakers and gurus who produce numerous seminars, books, and audio programs for the true believers who think they can attract success through positive thoughts. Other popular authors and books include:

- Keith Harrell   *Attitude is Everything*
- Napoleon Hill and   *Success Through a Positive*
  W. Clement Stone   *Mental Attitude*
- Dr. Norman Vincent Peale   *The Power of Positive Thinking*
                                      Six Attitudes for Winners
- Anthony Robbins   *Personal Power*
                                      Unlimited Power
                                      Awaken the Giant Within
                                      Live With Passion
                                      Money, Master the Game
- Dr. Robert H. Schuller   *You Can Become the Person*
                                      You Want to Be
                                      The Be Happy Attitudes
- Dale Carnegie   *How to Win Friends and*
                                      Influence People
- Rhonda Byrne   *The Secret*
- Les Brown   *Live Your Dream*
- Joel Osteen   *You Can, You Will*
                                      Become a Better You
                                      Your Best Life Now
- David Schwartz   *The Magic of Thinking Big*
- Zig Ziglar   *How to Get What You Want*

- Og Mandino   ***Secrets of Success***
- Brian Tracy   ***Bull's Eye: The Power of Focus***
                              Create Your Own Future
                              Eat That Frog!
                              Maximum Achievement
                              No Excuses!
- Steve Chandler   ***100 Ways to Motivate Yourself***
                              Reinventing Yourself
                              Crazy Good
- Bay and Macpherson   ***Change Your Attitude***

As you will quickly discover, a positive attitude that focuses on the future is one of the most powerful motivators for achieving success. Any of these recommended books will get you started on the road to changing your attitudes as well as your life. They are filled with fascinating stories of self-transformation, motivational language, and exercises for developing positive attitudes for success.

For a powerful alternative to the popular pseudoscientific positive thinking and laws of attraction approaches, see Richard Bandler's ground-breaking neuro-linguistic programming approach:

> Get the Life You Want: The Secrets to Quick and
> Lasting Change With Neuro-Linguistic Programming

Here's an important life-changing tip: Get serious about shaping your future by committing yourself to reading at least one of these books over the next two weeks. If reading is a problem for you, try to find audio programs that include similar material. You can find the books and audio programs in many libraries. Set aside at least one hour each day to read a book or listen to a program that can literally change your life. Such books and programs will both exercise your mind and inspire you to be your best!

BARRIER #27
Rude, disrespectful, and inconsiderate

QUESTIONS: Are you sometimes rude, disrespectful, and inconsiderate to others? Have you said things that cause you embarrassment? Do others try to avoid you or leave you out of conversations and meetings because of your toxic personality? Do you have difficulty setting boundaries and defining personal space? Do you make others feel uncomfortable in your presence? Are you the last one to be chosen to participate in projects, team efforts, or social events? Do you talk about yourself a lot, but no seems to listen?

IF NO: Move on to the next barrier. However, many people are oblivious to such negative behaviors and thus don't understand they are being silently ostracized by those they interact with. Violating their personal space and finding you irritating, they wish you would go away forever. Ask yourself these questions: Do you violate personal space by conducting conversations within 12 to 24 inches of other people's faces? Are you a "light listener" who often interrupts when someone else is talking? Do you try to dominate conversations? Do you enter an office without knocking or making an appointment? Do you use your cell phone for personal business while working with others? Do you talk loudly when others are trying to work? Do you make inappropriate jokes or comments to members of the opposite sex? Do you make negative comments to others about your boss? Do you tell your boss that you don't have time to do the assigned work or talk down to him or her? Do you dress differently from others in the company? Do you ask personal questions that are none of your business? Do you try to put other people down in efforts to build yourself up?

IF YES: No one wants to work with someone who is rude, disrespectful, or inconsiderate. Rude employees are generally disliked by other employees who prefer not working with them. Rude and inconsiderate employees also alienate customers who will take their business elsewhere. If you have a pattern of rudeness and disrespect, you need a social and psychological makeover.

TIPS: People like individuals who are polite and considerate, observe social graces, ask good questions, and have important things to say. Carefully watch what you say and when and where you say it. Since it's impolite to interrupt other people, wait until others are finished before you begin talking. Better still, become a good listener – you'll learn more by listening than by talking! If you have something important to ask or tell someone, do so privately rather than distract others in the office with loud and disruptive conversation. Be polite by knocking on doors and asking permission before entering offices with closed doors.

You might be a good candidate for a Dale Carnegie course related to his classic book ***How to Win Friends and Influence People***. You need to acquire some important people skills so that others will like you rather than avoid you. In addition to the Dale Carnegie book, examine a few of these people-sensitive titles:

- *The Fine Art of Small Talk*
- *How to Be a People Magnet*
- *How to Make People Like You in 90 Seconds or Less*
- *How to Start a Conversation and Make Friends*
- *How to Talk So People Listen*
- *How to Talk to Anyone*
- *Talking to Yourself*

BARRIER #28
Shy and introverted

QUESTIONS: Do you feel uncomfortable meeting strangers, engaging in small talk, and sustaining conversations? Do you understand how to network but prefer not engaging in this activity? When invited to a party or social hour, do you feel uncomfortable mingling with others and keep an eye on your watch and the exit door? Would you rather be at home instead of attending meetings? Do you get nervous getting up in front of a group to speak? Are you generally a shy person who prefers staying in the background rather than standing out front?

IF YES: One of the biggest roadblocks to both job search and on-the-job success is the failure to network properly. Networking is especially easy for highly extroverted and socially active individuals, but many shy and introverted people simply avoid situations that would require them to meet strangers and strike up conversations. They don't know how to build, maintain, and expand networks of personal and professional relationships that are keys to success. The engage in **negative self-talk** that directs them away from positive engagements and productive relationships.

TIPS: If you are shy and introverted (most people claim they are), you can still become an effective networker by learning some **basic people skills** that focus on building, maintaining, and expanding networks. These involve informational interviews, developing communication skills, and networking for information, advice, and referrals. Many job seekers have a clear understanding of the networking process – its central importance, how it works, and how to do it – but they fail to organize and implement an effective networking campaign. They may get started by contacting a few friends for information, advice, and referrals, but they soon fall back on old habits that seem less risky and more assuring – responding to job postings with resumes and letters. Part of this reluctance to engage in an active networking campaign goes back to some cultural issues related to childhood – parental admonitions not to talk to strangers nor be too assertive or personal among friends. Many people also are reluctant to make cold calls because they fear encountering rejections. And still other engage in negative self-talk that talks them out of taking initiatives that are in their best interests. If these are issues preventing you from developing an effective networking campaign in your job search, I recommend the following books to help you develop the necessary skills and motivation to network:

- *Dig Your Well Before You're Thirsty*
- *Fine Art of Small Talk*
- *A Foot in the Door*
- *How to Work a Room*
- *Make Your Contacts Count*
- *Masters of Networking*
- *Networking for People Who Hate Networking*
- *Never Eat Alone*
- *One Phone Call Away*
- *The Power to Get In*
- *The Savvy Networker*
- *Self-Promotion for Introverts*
- *Social Networking for Career Success*
- *Work the Pond*

The following websites also provide a wealth of information on the networking process for job seekers:

- **Quintessential Careers**   www.quintcareers.com/networking.html
- **Riley Guide**   www.rileyguide.com/netintv.html

- **My Career Transition**   mycareertransitions.com
- **Susan RoAne**   www.susanroane.com

BARRIER #29
Unwilling to learn and change behavior

QUESTIONS: Do you know what your weaknesses are and what you need to do to change your behavior? Do you have certain habits that drag you down or prevent you from becoming successful? Do you want to break those habits and replace them with new habits for success? Do you avoid learning new things that might help you improve your employability? Would you rather watch television and play games on your computer than take a course or read a book that could improve your education and strengthen your skills?

IF NO: Move on to the next barrier. However, be honest with yourself. We all have weaknesses and habits that may work against our best interests. Some of them may be barriers to job and career success.

IF YES: You can break habits and change your behaviors. But you first must **want** to make such changes. If, for example, you are overweight, you definitely should try to lose weight. It will be good for your health, appearance, and psychological well-being. But how difficult is it to lose weight? Theoretically, losing weight is not really difficult – you just have to eat less and exercise more; consume more protein and less carbohydrates; take in fewer calories as well as expel more calories. But few people have the will power to change their long-entrenched eating and exercise habits on their own. Some periodically go on a diet, join a weight loss group, or hire a personal coach to help them diet and exercise. Unfortunately, most people cannot sustain their weight loss, because they revert to old eating and exercise habits after undergoing a proverbial "training high." Some are dealing with deeper psychological issues, such as depression or other personal demons, and use food to blot out their problems. Most overweight people simply are not motivated to change their behaviors unless something major happens to them – they hit "bottom" – to significantly rewire their thinking. Sometimes a near death or spiritual experience, such as a heart attack, stroke, or celestial vision, will motivate them to significantly alter their behavior and make permanent lifestyle changes. But in the absence of compelling motivators, most people repeat their same old behavioral patterns. Unfortunately, there is little hope for the hopelessly addicted!

In many respects, losing weight is analogous to finding and keeping a job. Many people continue using the job-finding habits that don't work well – primarily respond to job postings, write mediocre resumes and letters, avoid networking, fail to prepare for interviews, prematurely ask about salary and benefits, and don't follow up after an interview. Once on the job, they may fall into the habits of shirking responsibility, conducting personal business on company time, and avoiding taking initiative. They present an image of someone who just wants to clock hours and pick up a paycheck without contributing much to the organization.

In today's fast-paced workplace, employees are expected to be responsible, take initiative, and acquire new skills through education and training. They are expected to be productive members of a team that is focused on achieving the goals of the organization.

TIPS: Be honest with yourself by compiling a list of habits and behaviors that work for and against you. If you have difficulty doing this, find a friend or family member who knows you well and ask them to identify your strengths and weaknesses. Ask them to candidly answer these questions about you:

1. What are my strengths?
2. What weak areas might I need to improve?
3. In your opinion, what do I need in a job or career to make me satisfied?

While we all have weaknesses we would like to improve, when it comes to finding and keeping a job, you should focus on your **strengths**. Employers want to hire your strengths rather than cope with your weaknesses. It's your strengths that add value to the organization. The following books offer a great deal of advice on how to best change your behavior and acquire new habits of success:

- *7 Habits of Highly Effective People*
- *The 10 Dumbest Mistakes Smart People Make*
- *The 12 Bad Habits That Hold Good People Back*
- *Change Your Attitude*

- *Change Your Brain, Change Your Life*
- *Change Your Job, Change Your Life*
- *Changing For Good*
- *The Habit Change Workbook*
- *Now, Discover Your Strengths*
- *Reinventing Yourself*
- *Simple Steps to Impossible Dreams*
- *The Success Principles*

BARRIER #30
Lack of energy and enthusiasm

QUESTIONS: Do you lack energy and enthusiasm when you speak with others? Do you often appear haggard, overworked, and depressed? Do you look 10 years older than you are?

IF YES: Employers want to hire people who are energetic and enthusiastic. However, if you lack goals and purpose and have negative attitudes and are somewhat depressed, you may present an unenthusiastic and tired image. Projecting energy and enthusiasm is especially important during a job interview and when dealing with clients.

TIPS: Talk to yourself in a mirror, using a reccording device. Energetic and enthusiastic people project their voices, speak in complete and coherent sentences, use terminology that is positive and future-oriented, and are active and supportive listeners. They also exhibit positive nonverbal behaviors: smile, maintain good eye contact, sit erect and with a slight forward lean, and use gestures to emphasize or dramatize points. Pay particular attention to the quality of your voice and how you respond to others. Listen carefully to what is being said or asked and respond with interest.

BARRIER #31
Lack clear focus

QUESTIONS: Are you easily distracted? Do you often feel overwhelmed and thus unable to get things done? Do you fail to set priorities and complete them accordingly? Do you find multitasking to be difficult? Do you tend to have a short attention span? Do you have difficulty reading long articles or a book? Do you lack a daily plan of action or a "to do" list that helps you set your agenda for the day? Do you spend a great deal of time surfing the Internet, checking your email, and using your cell phone? Do you let personal matters interfere with your work? Do you think you might have ADD or ADHD?

IF YES: In today's fast-paced and technologically sophisticated workplace, many people have difficulty keeping focused on what's really important in their work. Often required to multitask and be responsive, and frequently interrupted with unexpected demands, they become overwhelmed with trying to complete their work. At the end of the day, they feel tired and leave work with a sense of having dealt with chaos rather than accomplishing anything important.

TIPS: Your lack of focus can be a function of several things. First, it could be a result of the nature of your job – too much multitasking. Jobs have a tendency to grow beyond their actual descriptions and acquire excessive demands. In some cases, people are doing two different jobs that really should be done by different people. Take a good look at your daily routines. Are you doing more than what the job requires? Perhaps you need to meet with your boss to discuss how to better define your job. Second, this lack of focus could be a result of your own work habits, or the lack thereof. Are you well organized? Do you follow good time management practices? Do you let personal matters (Internet and telephone usage) interfere with your work? If so, you may be a good candidate for reorganizing your time, setting new priorities, de-cluttering your workspace, or changing employers. Third, like millions of other people, you may have attention deficit disorder (ADD) or a learning disability exacerbated by today's many competing technologies and communication forums – computers, tablets, smart phones, television, Internet, and email. If you think you might have adult ADD, examine some of these books:

- *ADD/ADHD Checklist*
- *Complete Learning Disabilities Handbook*
- *Delivered From Distraction*
- *Dr. Bob's Guide to Stop ADHD in 18 Days*
- *Driven to Distraction*
- *The Gift of Dyslexia*
- *Learning Outside the Lines*

- *New Hope for People With Bipolar Disorder*
- *Overcoming Dyslexia*
- *Surviving Manic Depression*
- *Taking Charge of ADHD*
- *You Mean I'm Not Lazy, Stupid, or Crazy?*

BARRIER #32
Lack goals, a sense of purpose, or a mission in life

QUESTIONS: Do you lack goals and a sense of purpose? Do you find yourself moving aimlessly through life, not sure what you want to do or accomplish? Do you frequently ask yourself, *"Is there more to life than this?," "Do I really want to continue doing this for the next five to 10 years?,* or *"What's my purpose or mission here on earth?"* Do you sometimes think *"I'm not sure what I want to do with my life"*? These are existential questions that we all face at various stages in our lives.

IF NO: Move on to the next barrier, but be prepared to re-address this barrier at times during your life. Many people who once had a clear vision of what they wanted to do undergo changes in goals and purposes. You, too, may eventually go through uncertain times and will ask yourself, *"What do I want to do with the rest of my life?"*

IF YES: Like many other people who go through different seasons of life, your goals and purposes may change at various stages of your life. Many young people, for example, may not know what they want to do with the rest of their lives. After gaining some work experience, and learning what they **don't** want to do, they formulate clearer goals, which tend to relate to specific jobs and careers. But later on, at mid-career, their goals may become more personal – related to family, community, and/or leisure. As they approach retirement age, their goals may focus more on having an impact on others or leaving a legacy behind. Without goals or a purpose, you may wander aimlessly in the job market as well as on the job. You may lack energy and enthusiasm and the motivation to be productive. Your future may be endangered because you lack direction in your career and your life. Purpose-driven people tend to enjoy life and look forward to each day with renewed energy.

TIPS: Developing goals and a purpose in life is easier said than done. There are many exercises you can complete that will help you develop goals and focus on your purpose and legacy in life, and develop a mission statement. I outline some of the most thorough-going such devices in my self-assessment book, *I Want to Do Something Else, But I'm Not Sure What It Is*. Get started by answering this question as thoroughly as possible:

What do you want to do with the rest of your life?

Then, write a hypothetical obituary and/or a "legacy will" for the year 2030. Identify your major accomplishments or those things that represent your best life and what nonmaterial things you want to be noted for.

I also recommend the following books, which will help you set goals and define your purpose in life:

- *7 Habits of Highly Effective People*
- *Become a Better You*
- *Choices That Change Lives: 15 Ways to Find More Purpose, Meaning, and Joy*
- *Claiming Your Place at the Fire*
- *How to Find Your Mission in Life*
- *I Will Not Die an Unlived Life: Reclaiming Purpose and Passion*
- *Life Reimagined: Discovering Your New Life Possibilities*
- *A Life You Were Born to Live: A Guide to Finding Your Life Purpose*
- *Live Your Calling: A Practical Guide to Finding and Fulfilling Your Mission in Life*
- *Man's Search for Meaning*
- *The Monk Who Sold His Ferrari*
- *A New Earth: Awakening to Your Life's Purpose*
- *Perfecting Your Purpose: 40 Days to a More Meaningful Life*
- *Plato and Platypus Walk Into a Bar*
- *The Power of Intention: Learning to Co-create Your World Your Way*
- *The Power of Purpose: Creating Meaning in Your Life and World*
- *The Promise: God's Purpose and Plan for When Life Hurts*
- *The Purpose-Driven Life*
- *Repacking Your Bags*
- *The Rhythm of Life: Living Every Day With Passion and Purpose*
- *Success is Not an Accident: Change Your Choices, Change Your Life*

- *Work Reimagined: Uncover Your Calling*
- *Your Life Calling: Reimagining the Rest of Your Life*

If you're interested in developing a mission statement that incorporates your goals and purpose in life, you're well advised to visit the following websites for tips on how to do so:

- www.nightinggale.com
- www.missionstatements.com
- www.timethoughts.com
- www.quintcareers.com/mission-statement-exercises/

BARRIER #33
Lack flexibility

QUESTIONS: Are you inflexible? Are you unwilling to consider other people's points of view, or compromise? Do you tend to barge ahead with your ideas and win at all costs? Do you sometimes alienate others because of your unwillingness to listen, empathize, and compromise?

IF YES: Inflexible people tend to quickly create conflict, generate enemies, and become loners. While they may rationalize their behavior as "leadership," they are not team players who can persuade others to follow their lead. The art of persuasion involves compromise – a willingness to see the other person's point of view and view problems from different perspectives. It often involves collective decision-making where everyone feels they had a part in the process.

TIPS: Begin by slowing down when you deal with other people. Decisions are all about managing relationships – take the time to nurture your relationships. Listen more to others' ideas and discuss your ideas rather than force them onto others. Rather than say, *"We should....,"* present your ideas for discussion by asking, *"What do you think about....?"* Asking good questions for setting the agenda and leading the discussion, rather than declaring conclusions and stifling competing points of view, will go a long way toward building your leadership skills.

BARRIER #34
Lack sense of entrepreneurism

QUESTIONS: Do you tend to do things the way you and others have always done them? Do you seldom think outside the box and come up with innovative approaches? Do you avoid taking risks?

IF YES: Effective job seekers tend to be very entrepreneurial. Rather than sit around waiting for jobs to come to them, they take a great deal of initiative to ensure that employers know about their qualifications. They become effective networkers who are willing to make many cold calls and use their contacts for conducting informational interviews and developing job leads. Once on the job, they become star employees because of their willingness to take initiative and solve problems. They develop a reputation as someone who can be relied on to come up with good decisions, implement, and follow through. They get called upon to play important roles in key decision-making because of their entrepreneurial skills.

TIPS: Try to reorient your mindset by becoming more creative and action-oriented. If you are looking for a job, initiate an active networking campaign that focuses on making cold calls and activating your network of relationships for the purpose of finding a job. You also should evaluate your approach to job hunting and consider alternative approaches that might yield better results. On the job, you need to focus on taking greater initiative in solving problems. Employers especially value employees who are self-directed rather than those who require direction and supervision. Begin your day by asking yourself this question:

> *What one thing can I do today, which is not part of my job description, that would improve the operations of my company?*

This one thing could involve saving money, improving profitability, or streamlining operations.

BARRIER #35
Appear lazy

QUESTIONS: Are you lazy? Do you try to avoid work? Do you show a lack of interest in work? Do you basically put in time rather than use your time wisely to further the goals of the company? Do you look for jobs that don't involve much work?

IF YES: You may be best fit for low-paying and sedentary jobs that don't involve much work – a night security guard or a shipping and receiving clerk in a company with little incoming or outgoing traffic. Some people appear lazy simply because they don't enjoy what they are doing – just putting in time to collect a paycheck and get benefits. Employers want to hire individuals who are energetic and who can contribute to achieving the goals of the company. If you have to be closely supervised and told what to do in order to get you to do anything, don't expect to keep your job very long. Employers can't afford such "expensive" employees.

TIPS: Start approaching your job in more basic economic terms – your talent in exchange for the employer's money. If you're making $10, $20, or $30 an hour, are you producing a sufficient level of goods and services to justify your salary and benefits? If you primarily work to put in time, chances are you are getting few on-the-job rewards. In addition, you are probably unhappy with your work. This may be a good time to take stock of your interests and skills and start looking for a job that is a better fit. If you find a job you really love, you'll be energized and focused. To find the kind of work you'll be happier doing, start by conducting a self-assessment. There are many self-assessment devices in *I Want to Do Something Else, But I'm Not Sure What It Is*.

BARRIER #36
Tactless and insensitive

QUESTIONS: Are you tactless and insensitive in dealing with other people? Are your relationships all about "me" rather than "us"? Do you try to win at any cost, which may mean trampling on the sensitivities of others?

IF YES: People want to work with others they like. Indeed, **likability** is one of the most important ingredients to getting hired as well as to advancing on the job. Tactless and insensitive individuals are usually shunned by their bosses, co-workers, and clients.

TIPS: Be especially sensitive to others in everything you do. Rather than always focus on "me," orient yourself to "you" and "us." Always follow the Golden Rule in relationships: *Do unto others as you would have them do unto you.*

BARRIER #37
Wear body art that sends negative messages

QUESTIONS: Are you a walking advertisement for tattoos and body piercings that translate into possible bad behavior or cause people to question your good judgment and mental health? Do your tattoos and piercings draw unusual attention to you? Are you trying to apply for jobs where such body art may be unacceptable? Did you at one impulsive time get some stupid tattoos in the wrong places that you wish could be removed? Do you think your body art is real cool?

IF YES: Remember that guy or gal you fell in love with and then got a tattoo to express your commitment? Whatever happened to him or her? And the tattoo? If you think your tattoos are really cool, guess what others think about you for having made the decision to get those tattoos?

Whether you like it or not, body art still tends to send negative messages to many employers – about your judgment and behavior. Perhaps it's a sign of an undiagnosed mood disorder issue, such as depression, anxiety, and impulsivity. At the same time, tattoos and body piercings are increasingly acceptable to many tolerant employers, as long as they don't interfere with job performance. In some occupations, such as in construction, the circus, music, art, and blue-collar jobs with high turnover, low pay, and minimum customer contact, even heavy tattooing and body piercing are acceptable. However, in many other jobs, which require a more conservative and professional image, extreme body art is unacceptable, especially if it indicates possible gang affiliations and negative messages.

TIPS: Be very careful about displaying your body art both during a job interview and on the job. The focus should be on your **qualifications** to do the job rather than on your artistic body image. If you display tattoos that will turn off potential employers, especially neck and head tattoos that cannot be easily covered, consider getting those tattoos removed as soon as possible. They will not enhance your employability. Rather, they will attract rejections like a magnet. Check with your local tattoo shop for information on how to remove extreme body art. Other tattoos on arms, legs, shoulders, and more private areas can be easily covered by clothing. Above all, you should not let youthful tattooing indiscretions interfere with your employability. Again, you want employers to focus on your job performance rather than on your body art and personal judgments about your self image.

BARRIER #38
Project a negative image

QUESTIONS: Do you tend to turn off people by how you look and what you say? Are you often unhappy with the image you project to others? Do you look too young, too old, too ill, too unhappy, too perky, too over-qualified, or too under-qualified to get the job as well as do the job?

IF YES: You can project a negative image in many different ways: dress, speech, and in writing (resume, application, letters). During the job search, prospective employers look for red flags and other clues for why they shouldn't hire you. This could be (1) the way you talk during a telephone screening interview (high pitched voice, grammatical errors, revealing words and phrases, listening skills, use of negatives, lack of enthusiasm and energy), (2) your writing style (organization, spelling, punctuation, and grammatical errors), (3) how you dress and handle yourself both verbally and nonverbally, and (4) what you reveal or omit on your resume (time gaps, job hopping, spelling errors, salary history, unrelated experience, lack of goals and focus). Once on the job, you must avoid similar negative images, especially how you deal with bosses, co-workers, and customers/clients.

TIPS: Remember, employers want to make the right hiring decision – find someone who can consistently come to work on time, take initiative, and do the job. They don't want to acquire new personnel problems that require a lot of wasted time and money to resolve. If you can't project a positive image to employers, don't expect to be hired or remain on the job for long. Take stock of how you write, speak, and comport yourself. Are you presenting your best self? How can you improve your image? It may be worth spending a little money to hire a career coach who can analyze your image and provide needed guidance on how you can improve your image. I outline numerous red flags, errors, and negative image issues related to the job search in the following books:

- *Job Interview Tips for People With Not-So-Hot Backgrounds*
- *No One Will Hire Me!*

■ *Resume, Application, and Letter Tips for People With Hot and Not-So-Hot Backgrounds*

BARRIER #39
Lack good interpersonal skills

QUESTION: Do you lack good interpersonal skills? Do you have difficulty making and keeping friends? Do some people dislike you at work? Do you often feel left out of the group? Do you sometimes feel awkward in social settings – not sure what to say or do? Do you prefer avoiding social functions that involve meeting strangers? Do you prefer staying home to going out and mingling with people?

IF YES: The ability to interact well with others in social situations and within the work setting is important both to landing a job and later to receiving promotions. Employers want to hire people who can work together to accomplish tasks for the overall good of the organization. Companies value employees who will pitch in to help someone else finish a project if there is a deadline looming. On the other hand, employees who say *"That's not my job"* or any of the other excuses revealed in Barrier #17 (page 34) are often expendable. The ability to work in harmony with others to get the work accomplished, but without spending a lot of time "chatting" about things other than the work, are remembered when it comes time for promotions or to decide who stays and who goes in times of cutbacks.

TIPS: When in the work setting, primarily confine your conversations with your co-workers to topics related to the projects you are working on and an agenda that relates to getting the job done. Although you are certainly expected to be friendly with the people you work with, there is a difference between being friendly and being friends. *"Good morning"* and *"How are you this morning?"* are certainly fine, but a long discussion of everything that happened over the weekend surely goes far beyond what the boss considers appropriate on "company time." Avoid any conversations, whether initiated by you or by others, that could be construed to be gossip. Gossip, though it happens frequently, has no place in the workplace. Social conversations can take place during break and the lunch hour.

If you will be attending social functions, whether as part of your job or not, you may want to read the following books that focus on developing relationships:

- *The Art of Small Talk*
- *How to Make People Like You in 90 Seconds or Less*
- *How to Start a Conversation and Make Friends*
- *How to Talk to Anyone*
- *How to Win Friends and Influence People*
- *How to Work a Room*

5

Health, Wellness, and Disabilities as Barriers

*"Physical and mental health issues are red flags for employers. If you have issues, try to reassure employers that your health situation will not affect your performance. Bad things may happen to good people, but **trust and honesty** define long-term relationships."*

THE ACTUAL OR APPARENT state of your physical and mental health can work in your favor or be a red flag to a prospective employer. Why, you might ask, does the employer care about your health? Disclose the fact that you are pregnant, bipolar, schizophrenic, have fibromyalgia, chronic fatigue syndrome, or Lyme disease, were recently diagnosed with cancer, or are HIV positive, and you'll raise some **big** red flags with many employers who may view you as high risk, costly to maintain, and potentially unproductive. If you look overweight, pale, and lethargic and have dull nails, circles around your eyes and yellow teeth, you may send negative messages about the state of your health and ability to be a productive employee. After all, employers want to hire healthy and energetic individuals who will be focused on workplace productivity rather than on their personal health issues.

Here's an interesting fact of today's worklife – **"presenteeism"** (employee presence at work) is more responsible for productivity losses than absenteeism. Indeed, many on-the-job mental health issues are responsible for low productivity among employees, especially depression, anxiety, and other mood disorders, which may also be complicated by drug and alcohol abuse.

There are several reasons why an employer may be reluctant to hire an individual who appears to have major health issues, especially chronic health problems. Poor physical or mental health might mean the applicant could not do the work. Certainly some types of work would pose greater problems than others. For example, in some instances work that is physically demanding might not get done. In other situations work might not be done in a timely manner or by a deadline might not be met because of absenteeism resulting from health issues.

If you have mental health problems, such as bipolar disorder, frequent depression, high anxiety, extreme anger, emotional instablility, or impulsive behaviors, you may have difficulty doing the work. Furthermore, the employer may regard you as posing a potential threat to co-workers and clients.

Beyond the question of whether a potential employee's health would be a detriment to the work being accomplished, many employers also have concerns as to how an employee in poor health might affect rising medical insurance premiums. With the annual cost that employers pay for employee medical insurance skyrocketing, employers, especially small business owners, are very wary of how their employees' excessive use of the health care system impacts their bottom line.

Keep in mind that one's perception of reality **is** reality to that individual. If you **appear** to be in poor health, whether you actually are or not, you will leave a negative impression of yourself with the interviewer. So your **appearance** of good health is as important to your chance of landing most jobs, as is the **actual state** of your health. Don't let the appearance of poor health be a barrier to landing a job you want.

Do what you can to maintain or improve your health. Certainly this is important to the overall quality of your life – not just to enhance your job opportunities. But don't stop there. Take a long, hard look at yourself in the mirror – head to toes. How might a stranger evaluate both your physical and mental health? Do you stand (as well as sit) straight and tall, or do you slouch? Do you look overweight, which might suggest health issues relating to heart disease and diabetes? Do you smile and exude energy and enthusiasm, or do you appear unhappy, tired, disinterested, or depressed? Do you have a sparkle in your eyes or do your eyes appear dull and lifeless? Do your teeth look healthy or do they indicate possible dental problems? Do you appear anxious and easily distracted? Some things that help you appear energetic and brimming with good health are related as much to your attitudes (see Barrier #26 on pages 45-50) as to the actual physical state of your health.

BARRIER #40
Have learning disabilities

QUESTIONS: Have you been diagnosed with Attention Deficit Disorder (ADD) or some other type of learning disability? Do you have difficulty concentrating? Does your mind sometimes wander aimlessly? Do you often mix up words and phrases? Do you or others sometimes think you're ignorant? Did you have learning problems in school? Do you have a hard time comprehending what you read and find reading a real chore?

IF YES: Even if you've not been diagnosed as having a learning disability, you may well have such a disability. Millions of people have difficulty concentrating, reading, and following instructions, because they suffer from ADD, ADHD, or dyslexia. A disproportionate number of high school dropouts, ex-offenders, and others who have difficulty getting and keeping jobs have learning disabilities that go undiagnosed and thus untreated. At the same time, many very successful and brilliant people also have had learning disabilities, including Albert Einstein and Ted Turner. If you've ever been dismissed from a job or received poor performance evaluations because you couldn't keep up with the work, you may have an undiagnosed learning disability. If diagnosed properly, these disabilities can be treated and you can begin channeling your work in more productive areas that emphasize your strengths rather than your weaknesses.

TIPS: If you suspect you have a learning disability, by all means see a professional who can assist you. Sometimes a change in diet or medication can help. But just knowing you have such a disability may help you better deal with issues related to your work. For more information on various types of learning abilities and what you can do to cope with them, see the recommended reading list under my earlier discussion of being focused in Barrier #31 (pages 56-57).

BARRIER #41
Experience difficult mental health issues

QUESTIONS: Have you been diagnosed as being bipolar? Do you exhibit signs of anxiety and stress? Do you have bouts of depression? Do you sometimes think other people are out to get you? Do you have a hard time controlling your emotions? Do you often get angry? Have you experienced rage? Could you benefit from anger management training?

IF YES: Mental health issues can have a devastating effect on the workplace. Individuals suffering depression, anxiety, and other mood disorders often have difficulty getting motivated and staying productive. People with bipolar disorder may have major mood swings that affect other employees. Angry individuals who become threatening and violent on the job can be very disruptive to the workplace. Most employers are ill equipped to deal with mental health issues. While some have employee assistance programs that provide mental health services, others prefer moving such employees out of the workplace altogether – make them as invisible as possible.

TIPS: Millions of working people experience severe depression, mood swings, anxiety disorders, and anger. Others are emotionally unstable, paranoid, or schizophrenic. All of these people can benefit from some form of professional help, be it therapy or counseling. Most mental illnesses also can be treated with medication. This is especially true in the case of depression, bipolar disorders, and schizophrenia. If you suspect you may have some mental health issues, by all means seek professional help. Most local hospitals offer mental health services, and many services are covered by health insurance. You may discover that your problems relate to a chemical imbalance that can be controlled with medication.

If you're in denial and hesitant to seek professional assistance, you might want to read a few books that will give you a better understanding of what you may be dealing with and how you can best get your life under control:

- *Bipolar Disorder*
- *Feeling Good Handbook*
- *Surviving Manic Depression*
- *Understanding Depression*

Identifying the mental health issue and admitting you have a problem will go a long way to getting it under control.

BARRIER #42
Appear overweight and unhealthy

QUESTIONS: Are you significantly overweight? Do you need to exercise more? Do you often feel sluggish? Do you have any weight-related health issues – blood pressure, heart, lungs? Would you like to lose 10 or more pounds? Have you tried dieting but with little success? Do you need help in better controlling your weight?

IF YES: Let's be honest – weight and body image are important issues for both employers and employees. If you are significantly overweight, you are probably tired of having people respond to you based in part on your appearance. You have probably tried to lose weight and flunked the exercise. Perhaps you have lost weight, only to put much or all of it back on. No doubt you believe it is unfair that your weight should be a significant factor in whether or not you get a job. If you can do the work required, that should be all that matters.

Perhaps that is the way the world should be. But it is not, and nothing good will come of your pretending differently or avoiding the subject. You can lament or rail at the unjustness of the situation, but that will not get you the job. In fact, many employers, especially small businesses, have other concerns about hiring overweight people – such employees may disproportionately have health problems that will negatively impact on the company's health insurance and absenteeism rates.

So what can you do? Obviously, an actual loss of weight would be a good step – for the sake of your health as well as enhancing your job prospects and self image. Theoretically, losing weight is not difficult. It's all about taking personal responsibility to regularly diet and exercise and being sufficiently motivated to take the necessary actions. But a successful outcome to weight loss is going to take some time, so if you need to land a new job soon, what other measures can you take?

TIPS: If you have a weight problem that won't go away soon, there are some things you can do immediately while you work on the longer term weight loss. For example, you can select clothing that de-emphasizes your weight – dark rather than light colors; stripes should run up and down, not around you; clothing should be loose fitting. Dress neatly and keep yourself well groomed.

Put on your best personality. Bright eyes that sparkle with enthusiasm, a sincere smile, and a voice that conveys interest and energy can make people forget – if they even notice – that the individual they are talking to is overweight. Stand, as well as sit, straight and tall with your shoulders back. Convey to the interviewer that you have the interest and the energy to do the work. Slouching will not hide your weight; it will be perceived as your lack of interest as well as make you appear lethargic. Employers are not anxious to hire lethargic individuals!

If asked about your biggest weakness (a favorite question of many interviewers) or something you wish you had done differently, seize the opportunity. Talk about (only if this is true) how you enjoy food so much that you let it get the better of you, and you put on a lot of weight. But you are taking action to change this. Discuss what action you have taken (fill in here the truth about you), such as joined a health club, purchased exercise equipment for your home, or you are running a mile each day. And you have already begun losing weight. In other words, you capitalize on the obvious (being overweight), and explain how you are taking action to change this negative to a positive. In fact, if you believe your weight is a major impediment to your being hired, you do not have to wait for the interviewer to ask a question such as the one above. At an appropriate moment you can bring it up. Just remember to emphasize the action you are taking to change the situation, and if you have already experienced success you can mention that too. After all, a job candidate who takes action for a positive change, and is successful, demonstrates qualities often sought by employers.

BARRIER #43
Smoke or use other addictive tobacco products

QUESTIONS: Do you smoke? Do you chew tobacco? Have you tried to quit smoking? Do you think it's unfair that employers discriminate against smokers and tobacco chewers?

IF YES: If you haven't gotten the message by now, you must be living under a rock! Smoking is **really, really, really bad** for your health. And secondhand smoke is really bad for those who are near you. Employers know the smoker stories all too well: Individuals who smoke have a disproportionate number of illnesses; they have higher absenteeism rates; and they have a negative impact on employers' health insurance rates. Smoking is a stupid habit that fewer and fewer employers feel compelled to tolerate. In fact, many employers simply will not hire smokers. Some will even fire smokers. Why hire such people? After all, smokers have a negative impact on the workplace. Expect to encounter many employers who run a smoke-free workplace populated by nonsmokers. If they learn that you smoke, they may look down upon you as someone who has a bad addiction and who might make stupid and self-destructive decisions. You simply won't get hired by many employers who feel this way.

TIPS: You've heard it numerous times. So here it is again: STOP SMOKING NOW! Similar to losing weight, when you stop smoking, you'll feel better, you'll live longer, you'll avoid the expensive health care system, and you'll get that job you want. If you feel you are hopelessly addicted to smoking, seek professional help to kick your addiction. Check with your local hospital for professional assistance or information on support groups that help members stop smoking. If you chew tobacco, you increase your chances of oral cancer. In addition, in the eyes of many people, you have a disgusting habit that really diminishes your image.

BARRIER #44
Lack cleanliness and good personal hygiene habits

QUESTIONS: Do you have any personal hygiene issues that could affect your employability? Do you often wear the same clothes over and over without laundering them. Do you neglect to bathe daily, brush your teeth regularly, use mouthwash, or apply deodorant? Are your fingernails unkempt? Do your shoes look worn and dirty? Do your clothes look old, torn, or dirty?

IF YES: Some readers may think these questions are silly, but, believe me, employers complain about individuals who arrive for an interview smelling "not so good." Some individuals have bad breath, while others have body odor – some have both. Why would this enter into a hiring decision of an otherwise "qualified" individual? The primary reason is that other employees do not want to work around a person who smells bad. This might not be as much of a deterrent if one is applying for an outdoor job, such as installing landscaping. But even then, the individual is likely to be riding in a truck to the job site with other crew members.

TIPS: Employers expect job applicants to present themselves well for the interview, and they don't expect that person's personal hygiene to improve once they are hired. Even for blue-collar physical labor jobs, interviewers expect, and prefer, applicants to be clean and neat in appearance. That means that clothing is clean and pressed; the person has bathed or showered that morning (done so a second time during the day if interviewing late in the day after a day of strenuous physical labor), deodorant has been used, teeth have been brushed and mouthwash is not a bad idea. There should be no "bad" smells. And watch the after-shave, cologne, or perfumes. If used at all, it should be lightly applied. The best impression is left when there is no odor to call attention to itself. If the interviewer remembers your cologne, you probably used too much. If there is any smell at all, let it be the faint smell of soap!

BARRIER #45
Appear haggard – too tired or in too poor health to do the work

QUESTIONS: Do you appear tired or/and haggard? Do you show your age more than other people – you're 28 but look 50? Do you wish you could look younger and more energetic?

IF YES: One dictionary defines "haggard" as "exhausted in appearance as from prolonged suffering or strain." Most of us probably feel tired from time to time, but to go to a job interview looking haggard is not putting one's best foot forward. Employers want to hire energetic people who will be able to put in a full day's work whether it be hard physical labor or bearing up well under the stress of a demanding office schedule. Individuals who look worn out may appear ill to others.

TIPS: Try to schedule your interview for a day of the week when you can get a decent night's sleep prior to the interview, and schedule for a time of the day when you will appear your most rested. Wear clothing that enhances your appearance of good health. For example, if you look great in fairly clear (bright, but not overly bright) shades of color, wear those shades rather than colors so toned down that you look dull and tired. However, if you look better in toned down shades, don't decide to put on bright colored clothing to "perk up" your appearance. It will overpower you, wash you out, and make you appear even more tired than you are.

Put energy into your voice. Speak enthusiastically about the things you have done as well as what you can do for the employer. Look alert with a facial expression that conveys your interest in the company and the job. Sit up straight on the chair with a very slight, almost imperceptible forward lean into the conversation with the interviewer. The appearance of energy and your enthusiasm will help you convey to the interviewer that you are neither too tired, nor in too poor health to do the work.

BARRIER #46
Have an obvious physical disability

QUESTIONS: Do you have a physical disability that is clearly apparent when you meet people? Do you have mobility issues that could raise questions about your ability to do the job? Will your hearing or sight limit you from doing certain jobs?

IF YES: You're not alone with such disabilities. More than 56 million Americans (19 percent of the population) are estimated to have some type of disability, physical or mental, many of which impact on the workplace. While people with disabilities have a high unemployment rate, once they are hired they tend to be excellent workers and loyal to employers who treat them fairly.

Certain disabilities are covered by the Americans With Disabilities Act (ADA). For information on this legislation, visit this gateway government website: www.dol.gov/dol/topic/disability/ada.htm

Other disabilities need to be addressed in a timely manner and in reference to the needs of employers. Don't just assume you are protected under the ADA and thus your disability will not be an issue in the hiring process. The ADA does not force any employer to hire a person with a disability if that person is not the most qualified candidate; even when the person is the most qualified, no law requires that he or she must be hired. All that is required is that the person be given "equal consideration" with other candidates.

The reality is that employers may have legitimate concerns about hiring a person with a disability. They may worry about the possible cost of job accommodations, whether the person will fit into their workplace, be able to work with a minimum of supervision, and so forth. They don't want to incur the possible additional costs – time, money, and lost opportunities – that are, fairly or unfairly, associated with accommodating persons with disabilities. However, numerous online resources are available for employers and for job seekers with disabilities. For information on ways to accommodate various disabilities in the workplace, see the website for the Job Accommodation Network: www.jan.wvu.edu.

Employers want to hire assets rather than incur possible new liabilities. Disability groups differ among themselves about when a job seeker with a disability should disclose his or her disability – during the interview or after getting the job. All persons with disabilities are familiar with the unfortunate issue of discrimination, and most have experienced it at one time or another, in one way or another, in the workplace.

TIPS: Be prepared to deal with the issue of your disability, with all its ramifications, by being positive and focused on the needs of the employer, not your own needs. Let the employer know they are hiring someone with the necessary skills, abilities, and motivation to get the work done, rather than merely hiring a disabled person. Tell your story, in as positive language as possible without exaggeration, about your past accomplishments/achievements, what you can do, and will do in the position you are interviewing for. Try to speak the language of employers and address their concerns about hiring the right candidate for the job.

Focus on your strengths and your willingness to learn and assume responsibilities, rather than your limitations. There are many ways employers can accommodate employees with disabilities, and studies show that most cost either nothing or a minimal amount. Educate yourself as much as possible on accommodations for persons with your particular type of disability and use that information in the interview if the issue of how you can do the functions of the job comes up.

While the employer cannot legally ask you flat out if you have a disability, nevertheless, he may view your disability as a barrier to employment. If he perceives that you have a mobility problem (for example), he can legally ask you **how** you would do the job. The ball would then be in your court, and the more familiar you are with methods of job accommodations and with the nature and functions of the job you are interviewing for, the easier it will be for you to reassure the employer than you **can** do the job and at minimal or no cost to him. You can give him a fact sheet from an organization that represents your disability, a list of websites containing relevant information, and a list of suitable references who are already familiar with your work skills and habits.

The same is true for other disabilities. Know your strengths and pursue jobs that require such strengths. Be prepared to deal with obvious disability issues during the job interview. While an employer may not ask you about your disability because of legal issues, nonetheless, he or she may view your disability as a barrier to your ability to do the job. Be prepared to deal with this unspoken objection to hiring you by volunteering the obvious. If asked, for example, what are your weaknesses, you might respond as follows:

> Some employers may think my mobility challenge will have a negative impact on the job. However, this has never been a issue with previous employers. In fact, I've learned to get around with no problems. The work I do does not require any special accommodations beyond what is normally found in the workplace. I've always exceeded the expectations of my employers and have become a valuable asset to everyone I work with. I just want to assure you that what you may consider a disability will not become an issue.

The point here is that disabilities are unspoken issues with many employers who see them as barriers to getting the work done. The more you can reassure a potential employer that you have overcome such barriers by providing evidence of your productivity and accomplishments related to your unique strengths, the more likely you will get the job. In so doing, you either neutralize a potential barrier to employment or turn it into a strength for getting the job.

The following books are designed to assist individuals with disabilities in overcoming barriers to employment:

- *Able to Work Job Outlook: A Special Needs OOH*
- *Disabilities/Different Abilities*
- *Employment Options*

- *I Am Potential*
- *I'd Rather Be Working*
- *Job Hunting for the So-Called Handicapped*
- *Job Search Handbook for People With Disabilities*

BARRIER #47
Have a history of chronic illness

QUESTIONS: Do you have a history of chronic illness or an autoimmune disease that prevents you from keeping a job for very long? Do you suffer a great deal of pain or have a history of recurring cancer? Do you have arthritis, asthma, COPD, hepatitis C, multiple sclerosis, heart disease, diabetes, lupus, Lyme disease, Parkinsons disease, fibromyalgia, chronic fatigue syndrome, a diabetic neuropathy, Crohn's disease, ulcerative colitis, or HIV/AIDS? Do you need to find a job that gives you full medical coverage? Are you unable to work full time? Have you ever lost or left a job because of your chronic condition?

IF YES: Over 125 million Americans are estimated to have some type of chronic condition! Many conditions, of course, are more serious than others – they become debilitating, demoralizing, and devastating as such individuals experience a combination of physical and mental conditions, such as excruciating pain, stress, anxiety, hopelessness, and depression. Many also have serious mobility issues as well as difficulty in building relationships and intimacy. Some conditions are so debilitating that they pose serious challenges for individuals who may have difficulty finding and keeping a full-time job as well as developing a successful career. This is one of those barriers to employment that you may have little control over. As a result, you appear to be a liability rather than an asset for many employers. People with chronic illnesses miss work, may appear ill at work, and treatment of their illnesses negatively impacts on the already high cost of employer-provided insurance. If one of your major needs is health benefits and you ask many questions about health insurance coverage, you may appear needy to employers. Your performance abilities must be exceptional to overcome this big red flag. Since many chronic conditions are considered disabilities and are thus covered by the Americans With Disabilities Act, you may have some legal recourse should you be discriminated against because of your condition, but this is often difficult to prove.

TIPS: Be prepared to encounter objections to hiring you because of your health condition. Many employers, especially small businesses, will have difficulties accommodating your health issues. Nonetheless, as long as you can do the job and your condition does not negatively impact on others, this should not become an issue. But should you disclose your chronic condition before being offered the job or wait until after you start the job? I recommend disclosure, but only during the negotiations or after you have been offered the job. If you disclose your condition early in the interview process, you unnecessarily raise a negative that may cloud an employer's view of your work-related abilities. But be careful how you disclose. Let the employer know this is a personal issue that you are dealing with and that it should not affect your work. If you don't disclose during the critical period between negotiations and starting the job, the employer may feel deceived once he or she later learns about your condition. It's important that you develop a good and trustworthy relationship with your employer from Day One.

At the same time, given a chronic physical condition, you may want to seek jobs that allow you flexible hours and the ability to work off-site. Telecommuting jobs may be ideal for you. However, finding an understanding and accommodating employer is the ideal situation for people with chronic conditions. Check out these two useful websites for assistance in handling such job search situations:

- www.chronicillnessturnaroundcoach.com
- www.CIcoach.com

PART III

Job Search Barriers You Can Change

6

Myths, Misunderstandings, and Your Mindset

"Many job seekers are their own worst enemies – they lack appropriate knowledge and skills to conduct an effective job search. Such self-inflicted employment barriers can easily be overcome through self-awareness and action."

S OME OF THE MOST IMPORTANT barriers to employment relate to the whole job search process – how one goes about looking for a job. Indeed, how you approach your job search largely determines whether or not you will land a job that's right for you.

It's no secret that many job seekers are their own worst enemies. Misunderstanding how the job market works and not knowing how to properly prepare for finding a job, they engage in numerous activities that produce less than stellar results. Preoccupied with looking for jobs through print and electronic job postings, for example, they fail to spend adequate time making cold calls, and networking for information, advice, and referrals – the most productive activities for getting job interviews. When it comes time to write resumes and letters, use social media, complete applications, interview for jobs, or negotiate terms of employment, they make many simple mistakes that have major consequences for their employability. They basically conduct a mediocre job search.

This chapter outlines numerous self-inflicted barriers to employment that mostly relate to the lack of knowledge and skills about the job market and how best to approach employers and conduct an effective job search. If you follow the relevant tips for each barrier, you should be able to quickly overcome some of the most important perceived difficulties to finding a great job and advancing your career. Once you overcome many of these job search barriers, you'll be well on the road to finding a job that's right for you!

BARRIER #48
Believe the job search process won't take long

QUESTIONS: Do you think you will be able to find a new job within a few days or weeks? Do you feel you can quickly convince employers to hire you?

IF YES: You may have an unrealistic view of how long it really takes to find a job in today's job market, or you may have decided to pursue low-paying jobs with a high turnover rate. On average, it takes from three to six months to find a job. Professionals with higher level education, skills, and salaries generally take longer to find a job than lower level professionals and blue-collar workers. Individuals who are likely to find a job in a very short period of time tend to look for low-paying, high-turnover jobs which are in high demand – jobs that few people want to keep for very long. For example, restaurants often have an 80 to 100 percent annual turnover of personnel! Many of these jobs, which require little background scrutiny, also are relatively open for people with not-so-hot backgrounds. Many minimum wage jobs in restaurants, construction, hospitality, food processing, landscaping, transportation, banking, and telemarketing offer opportunities for people who need to quickly find a job.

TIPS: If you are looking for a job that leads to a rewarding long-term career, modify your expectations by planning to spend several weeks, or even a few months, connecting with the right job. During that time you will probably experience many psychological ups and downs as you encounter rejections. You'll also learn a great deal about yourself and others if you organize an effective job search. But if you must quickly find a job, your best bet is to look for high-turnover, or what some call "stop-gap," jobs. Many of these jobs will not require a resume or a lengthy job interview. Just show up, complete an application, interview for the position, and get hired – often on the same day! But don't expect much in terms of compensation or view such jobs as having much of a career future. These are often dead-end, stop-gap, or "lifeboat" jobs which only a few people keep for very long.

Alternatively, you may want to contact several temporary employment firms that may be able to quickly place you in a variety of temporary jobs. Some of the largest ones with offices nationwide include Labor Finders, Manpower, Kelly Services, Olsten, Aerotek, and Robert Half:

- **Labor Finders**   www.laborfinders.com
- **Manpower**   www.manpower.com
- **Olsten**   www.olsten.com
- **Kelly Services**   www.kellyservices.com
- **Aerotek**   www.aerotek.com
- **Robert Half**   www.roberthalf.com

BARRIER #49
Think you can hide or embellish your past through deception

QUESTIONS: Do you have red flags in your background that you would rather not reveal to prospective employers? Do you think you can just change your past patterns of behavior through the force of willpower? Have you ever lied about yourself to others? Do you think you can hide your past without someone discovering what you did and who you really are? Have you ever thought of changing your identity? Do you make up stories about yourself in order to impress others?

IF YES: You are on a slippery slope with employers and possibly delusional about reality. The truth is that people with red flags in their background have few places to hide these days. Indeed, given today's increasingly sophisticated security and search technologies, employers increasingly conduct relatively inexpensive but thorough background checks on prospective employees that can reveal everything from your credit history to your criminal record. Even if you do hide or embellish your past, chances are your past will soon catch up with you and you'll be discovered as a fraud. When that happens, you'll probably be fired. Another truth is that few people can change their behavior through the force of willpower. Most people form **patterns of behavior or habits** that are difficult to alter unless they undergo some profound change that affects their motivation to engage in purposeful change.

TIPS: Honesty is always the best policy. Rather than try to hide your past, try to come to terms with it by being honest with yourself and those around you. If you've made mistakes, own up to them, and make the necessary changes so they don't recur. Be prepared to deal with objections to your background by putting together positive redemption and transformation "stories" about how you have overcome your past. Focus on what is right about you and how the "new you" will benefit the employer. I deal with this issue within the context of the job interview in *Job Interview Tips for People With Not-So-Hot Backgrounds* as well as in several job search and re-entry books designed for ex-offenders (see the resources featured on the home pages of www.impactpublications.com and www.exoffenderreentry.com). If you have a particularly difficult background (robbed or injured a previous employer, engaged in violent behavior, or convicted of a sex crime), you are well advised to see a professional counselor who can assist you with your special issues that may appear to be insurmountable barriers to employment.

BARRIER #50
Organize an ineffective and outdated job search

QUESTIONS: Are you unsure how to organize an effective job search? Does your job search plan involve a 10-step sequential process? Are you still doing the same things you did the last time you looked for a job?

IF YES: Few job seekers know how to organize an effective job search. Many start with writing their resume and then proceed to send it, along with a cover letter, in response to print and electronic job postings. Few have a clear employer-centered objective that states what they really want to do. And many don't know how to identify their skills, network, answer key interview questions, and negotiate salary and benefits. They wander haphazardly into today's competitive job market and quickly become frustrated and disillusioned by the meager results they generate from all their mailings to prospective employers.

TIPS: As illustrated on page 84, your job search should be organized as a 10-step process. Each step needs to be completed in the order outlined in this figure.

10 Steps to Job Search Success

10. Negotiate Salary and Benefits Like a Pro

9. Develop Winning Job Interview Skills

8. Network for Information, Advice, and Referrals

7. Write Effective Resumes and Letters

6. Conduct Research on Jobs, Employers, and Communities

5. State a Powerful Objective

4. Assess Your Skills and Identify Your MAS

3. Select Appropriate Job Search Approaches

2. Seek Assistance and Become Proactive

1. Examine and Change Your Attitudes

Unfortunately, many job seekers fail to understand each of these steps and how they relate to one another. They often start their job search with Step 7 – write resumes and letters – before knowing what they want to do (Step 5) or knowing what they do well and enjoy doing (Step 4). As a result, they tend to write awful resumes and letters that present a very weak picture of what they have done, can do, and will do in the future. In addition, their job search lacks a sense of purpose and direction. Such job seekers also tend to encounter numerous rejections because they simply don't know how to conduct an effective job search involving all of the 10 steps in their proper order.

Take, for example, Step 1, "Examine and Change Your Attitudes." This establishes the foundation for the remaining nine steps. Without the proper attitudes, which also affect your motivation and point you in the right direction, you will have difficulty completing the other steps. Step 4, "Assess Your Skills and Identify Your MAS," is one of the most important steps for completing Steps 5 through 10. Step 7, "Write Effective Applications, Resumes, and Letters," should come only **after** completing three preliminary preparation steps, including conducting research on individuals, organizations, communities, and jobs. Once you complete a powerful resume, you should be ready to execute the most important steps in your job search: (8) networking, (9) interviewing, and (10) negotiating salary and terms of employment.

I strongly recommend that you frequently refer to the diagram on page 84 throughout your job search. Be sure to take the time to complete each step thoroughly and in the proper order. If you do this, you will be well on your way to finding a job that is right for you. I provide details on the major job search steps in my comprehensive job search book, *Change Your Job, Change Your Life*.

BARRIER #51
Lack the financial wherewithal to sustain a lengthy job search

QUESTIONS: Are you unable to finance a two- to six-month job search? Would your financial situation become difficult if you remained unemployed for several months?

IF YES: You're not alone! Most people would soon become financially strapped if they had to go through a lengthy period of unemployment. Indeed, many people are already heavily indebted, and some live from paycheck to paycheck. Lose your job and you may soon lose your house, car, health insurance, and independence.

TIPS: For obvious financial reasons, don't quit your current job until you've located another job. After all, finding another job may take you several months during which time you need to meet your financial obligations. If you lose your job, as part of your separation, try to negotiate some type of severance package. This might include a month or two of additional salary and benefits, especially health insurance which can be very costly if you have to pay for it yourself. Also, consider finding a stop-gap job that would give you some income and benefits. Contact a temporary employment firm (see Barrier #48), which may be able to place you immediately into a temporary or permanent (many of these firms have temp-to-perm programs) position. If you need benefits, consider working part time at such firms as Starbucks, which are noted for extending health benefits to their many part-time employees. Such a job will give you the flexibility to continue your job search on a near full-time basis.

BARRIER #52
Heavily indebted

QUESTIONS: Are you spending more than you are earning? Are you heavily indebted? Are you concerned that your next job will not enable you to get out of debt? Do you need to substantially increase your income in your next job?

IF YES: You and millions of others have a similar problem. In fact, recent research shows that the rise in American indebtedness is largely due to major increases in the basic cost of living – housing, education, and transportation – rather than due to irresponsible or extravagant spending. Expect to continue your indebtedness unless something major happens to your income, such as a better paying job, an inheritance, or winning the lottery.

TIPS: Try saving more money by going on a financial diet – if you have more than two credit cards, get rid of them; cut down on unnecessary expenses, such as dining out, entertainment, and buying new cars every couple of years; and try to pay off as many debts as quickly as possible. See a financial planner who can help you better put your financial house in order. To get better control of your finances, read the following books:

- *9 Steps to Financial Freedom*
- *The Money Book for the Young, Fabulous, and Broke*
- *The Truth About Money*

At the same time, start looking for jobs that pay more than you currently earn. If you need to get additional education or training to qualify for such jobs, invest in yourself by getting the right degrees or certification. Research continues to show that one of the best returns on investment is education. The more education and training you acquire, the higher the salary you should be able to earn. Just make sure you're not getting education and training for jobs that can be easily outsourced or offshored!

BARRIER #53
Lack proper documentation

QUESTIONS: Do you lack documentation necessary for getting and keeping a job? Are you operating in a gray economy that doesn't require much documentation? Are you an ex-offender? Are you an undocumented (illegal) immigrant? Do you have the proper licenses or certificates to do the job?

IF YES: Most workers need some or all of the following documents: driver's license, birth certificate, and Social Security card. Others may need transcripts, licenses, certifications, citizenship papers, and health documents to qualify for certain jobs. Ex-offenders also need to get a copy of their rap sheet. If you lack such documents, you have a major problem in getting ahead in today's job market. As many illegal immigrants know, you can still find jobs (construction, hospitality, day labor centers) without proper documentation by purchasing false documents or by finding employers who don't ask questions about one's background. However, such employers often pay minimum wages and many take advantage of employees who are undocumented since they know few will take legal action to challenge their exploitation.

TIPS: Make sure you have proper documentation. If, for example, you are an ex-offender, see your parole or probation officer or contact a community corrections organization that can assist you. If you are an illegal immigrant, contact a group that can assist you with documentation. This may be a church, immigration lawyer, or a community-based immigrant advocacy group. In the past, periodically the federal government has offered amnesty to undocumented immigrants who take advantage of new documentation offers.

BARRIER #54
Look for jobs in the wrong places

QUESTIONS: Do you primarily look for print and electronic job postings? Do you spend most of your job search time sending resumes and letters and waiting for employers to contact you? Do you feel you could use some advice on improving your job search approach?

IF YES: Most job seekers waste a great deal of time engaged in wishful thinking. They believe most available jobs are represented in print and electronic job postings. As a result, they spend 80 percent of their time responding to such vacancy announcements with resumes and letters and then waiting to be contacted by employers for job interviews. Such activities give job seekers a false sense of making progress in the job market, because they believe they are doing something they think will result in a job. These also are the main job search activities of many frustrated job seekers who complain there no jobs available for them or that employers are not interested in hiring them. We hear this complaint again and again from job seekers who are primarily focused on finding employment through print and electronic job postings.

But the likelihood of landing a job this way is similar to being struck by lightning – very unlikely. In fact, these are the least effective places to look for employment. Known as the "advertised job market," because employers pay to have their job vacancies listed in these media, only about 15 percent of individuals find jobs through these formal job listing channels.

Research continues to confirm that most jobs – over 80 percent – are found on the "hidden job market." These jobs are found through word-of-mouth, networking, cold calls, knocking on doors, and direct application. Jobs found on the hidden job market also tend to be better paying, more secure, less competitive, higher quality, and more satisfying than those found on the advertised job market. Advertised jobs are disproportionately highly competitive, difficult-to-fill, and low-paying positions. After all, employers often have to advertise a job because they find it is difficult to fill through other less public means.

TIPS: You should spend most of your job search time focused on the hidden job market. If you are devoting more than 30 percent of your time looking for jobs through job postings, you are most likely wasting a great deal of job search time that could be put to more productive use by engaging in the most effective job search activities, especially networking and informational interviews. Your goal should be to get as many job interviews as possible – not to send out lots of resumes and letters in the hope of connecting to a few employers. As you will see when examining effective networking strategies, the fastest way to get job interviews is through networking for information, advice, and referrals.

Individuals with not-so-hot backgrounds should spend most of their job search time focused on the hidden job market. Networking and cold-calling activities enable them to be pre-screened by many individuals who will refer them to employers interested in their abilities and skills. Employers found on the hidden job market are less likely to rely on paper qualifications, which often accentuate red flags of applicants with difficult backgrounds. Through networking, you are screened more on the basis of face-to-face meetings and conversations, where what you say and do during the encounters are more important than what you have written in your resume, letters, and applications.

BARRIER #55
Approach the job search for negative reasons

QUESTIONS: Are you looking for another job because you dislike your present job? Did you get fired or laid off? Do you think the grass will be greener with another employer?

IF YES: Most people know what they don't like to do rather than what they like to do. People often quit their jobs because they are unhappy – frustrated with their boss or co-workers, didn't get a raise or promotion, felt unappreciated, bored with what they did – or they think the grass will be greener elsewhere. Those who get fired usually have a negative feeling toward their employer and job – they were unfairly let go or politically assassinated; they want to find a new job that will vindicate their previous situation. If asked why they are looking for a job, they may use negative terms – didn't like what they were doing, unhappy with who they were working for, or got fired or laid off. Probed further, they want this new job because they need the money and accompanying benefits. If you approach your job search from this perspective, chances are you will communicate your negativity to prospective employers. Few employers want to work with such people since they bring too much negative baggage to the job and company. Employers look for positive individuals who can produce positive results.

If you know what you don't like to do, you'll most likely try to avoid jobs that make you unhappy. But you won't know what really motivates you to excel and thus you will have difficulty communicating why you want a particular job. Take, for example, this question which employers often ask during a job interview:

Why should we hire you?

Can you give three positive reasons why someone would want to hire you? Are these reasons self-centered or employer-centered?

It will be to your advantage to change your orientation toward the job market by becoming more goal-oriented and positive. Once you discover what you do well and enjoy doing, and can formulate an employer-oriented objective, you will be well on your way to targeting a job and employer that will be right for your particular interests, skills, abilities, and motivation. Your whole outlook on and attitude toward the job search and prospective employers will become more positive. You'll be able to present a clear picture of what you really want to do – and do so in a very enthusiastic and energetic manner.

TIPS: Always have positive reasons for finding a job. Start by identifying what you want to do by developing a positive 30-word objective which will eventually appear on your resume and be the focus of your job interview. The best type of objective is oriented toward skills and results. It follows this format:

I would like a job where I can use my ability to _____, which

will result in _____ .
(outcome)

(your skill)

For example, at a general level, an objective that follows this format might be stated as follows:

> I would like a job where my experience in retail management, supported by strong sales/customer service experience, will result in excellent product displays and merchandising.

This general objective should be restated on a resume as a job-targeted objective:

> Retail Management position which will use sales/customer service experience and creative abilities for innovative product display and merchandising. Long-term goal: Become merchandise manager with corporate-wide responsibilities for product line.

I outline a process for identifying your motivated abilities and skills (MAS) and formulating a positive employer-oriented objective in *I Want to Do Something Else, But I'm Not Sure What It Is*.

BARRIER #56
Hang around the wrong people

QUESTIONS: Do you hang around people who tend to drag you down? Do you run with losers rather than winners? Do you have difficulty making friends with people who can help you find a job? Do you have difficulty networking for information, advice, and referrals?

IF YES: The best way to find a job is through other people rather than responding to advertisements or job postings. The same is true for advancing your career – you do so through other people who know you well, admire your performance, and like you. Your best approach will be to "spread the word," as well as your resume, to people who know you and who know others who might be interested in your qualification. The process I call networking involves acquiring information, advice, and referrals from others relating to your job and career objective. While many people understand the concept of networking, few actually invest the necessary time and effort to implement an effective networking campaign. This is unfortunate since networking remains the single most important approach to finding good-quality jobs on the hidden job market.

TIPS: Make sure you hang around the right people who can give you good information, advice, and referrals. These are quality individuals who may dispense useful advice and have good connections with others who can be helpful. These individuals might be relatives, former classmates and teachers, acquaintances, colleagues, neighbors, ministers, or even the postman or UPS driver. Take out your Christmas card list and identify individuals whom you believe might be helpful in finding a job. Don't be afraid to announce that you are looking for a job and would appreciate any information, advice, and referrals related to your job objective.

Share your resume with these individuals. You may be pleasantly surprised to discover how interested and helpful such individuals can be. Many of them will take a personal interest in your situation and give you a wealth of information, advice, and referrals. They will literally become your extra set of eyes and ears for locating jobs that best fit your employment profile. I outline the whole networking process in *The Savvy Networker: Building Your Job Net for Success*. Also see Barriers #79 and #80 (pages 122-129) on effective networking.

BARRIER #57
Fail to come to terms with a termination

QUESTIONS: Are you angry about your termination? Do you want to get even with those who terminated you? Do you have difficulty moving on with your life?

IF YES: Being fired is no fun. It has psychological consequences that can become debilitating if you don't rebound properly. It's an intensely personal and negative experience associated with everything from betrayal to injustice. Most terminated individuals go through the classic five stages of death and dying, from anger to acceptance. But you are not alone. Thousands of people get terminated every day. The important thing is to learn from the experience and move on with your life. Like most seasons in life, this, too, shall pass. Five years from now you may look back and say that this termination was the best thing that ever happened to you. You moved on to a much better and more rewarding job. The firing taught you what you didn't like to do as well as helped you clarify what you really wanted to do with the rest of your life. Indeed, it was a real eye opener!

TIPS: The good news is that there is life after termination – often much better than before. But you must make it happen, and it may take some time to make a positive transition. First, get over what happened to you by focusing on the future rather than replaying the past. Let go of the past as you change your whole attitude and motivation toward finding a new job or changing careers. Second, learn from what happened to you so you don't repeat the same scenario in future jobs. What lessons did you learn about yourself and others from that termination? Third, do all the job search basics – follow my 10-step job search process (see Barrier #50 on page 84), from changing your attitudes and identifying what it is you want to do to writing powerful resumes and letters, conducting research, and networking. Fourth, try to mend any negative relations with former employers. Since most future employers will check your previous employment record, you want to at least neutralize what could become negative references. Admit any errors you have made and thank your previous employers for the opportunity to learn and grow, even though things did not work out like both of you had hoped. Taking such "fence mending" actions and letting go of the past may prove to be some of the most important actions you take in putting yourself on the road to renewed career success.

BARRIER #58
Quit your job before being offered another job

QUESTIONS: Have you ever quit your job or informed your employer that you will probably be leaving soon before receiving a job offer from another employer? After being invited to a job interview, did you tell others that you would quit your job? Have you ever bragged to your co-workers about changing employers and making a lot more money?

IF YES: Don't prematurely assume you will be getting a job offer just because you were invited to an interview. While your chances of getting an offer may be good, you are still competing with other candidates and the employer may simply decide not to hire at all. If you begin telling others, including your boss, that you are leaving, your status as an employee may quickly change. The employer will most likely start looking for your replacement, increase your work load in preparation for your departure, and take you out of consideration for promotions, raises, or bonuses. After all, there is no reason to further invest in you since you've decided to leave. You are no longer a loyal and dependable employee.

TIPS: When it comes to your current boss and co-workers, conduct your job search quietly and be careful whom you talk with about your new job and career plans. While you may be excited about the prospect of getting another job and want to share your plans and any good news with others you work with, avoid this temptation. There is a proper time and place to announce your departure – when you have a firm job offer in writing from another employer and in the office of your current employer.

At that time, you should schedule a meeting with your employer and inform him or her of your decision to change jobs. Your employer might even make a counter offer in order to keep you. Also, be discreet in what you tell others about your new job. Some employees literally sabotage the workplace by bragging about what a terrific new opportunity they have and how much more money and benefits they will be receiving. While this may make you feel good, you'll probably make others feel bad. If your employer learns you are telling such stories, he or she may want to move you out of your job immediately, and you may damage your relationship, as well as future references, with your current employer.

Be professional in how you handle your departure. In the end, you will probably exaggerate the new job reality. And if you end up not getting the job after having announced your departure and bragged about how much you would be advancing your career, you will be embarrassed and you may become deadweight in the organization. You may even lose your job! After all, your employer has to now decide whether to take you back after having mentally said goodbye to you and perhaps hired someone else!

BARRIER #59
Lack effective online job search skills

QUESTIONS: Do you regularly use the Internet in your job search? Do you need to learn more about how to use the Internet for locating job opportunities and networking for information, advice, and referrals?

IF YES: If you're not using the Internet in your job search, you're missing out on many opportunities that can be easily accessed online. Indeed, both recruitment and the job search have increasingly incorporated the Internet. Over 50,000 websites include job listings. For job seekers, the Internet is especially useful for conducting research on jobs and employers, communicating by email, posting resumes online, and surveying job postings. Savvy job seekers know how to use the Internet for locating employers and acquiring useful information on all phases of their job search, from self-assessment and resume writing to networking and negotiating salary and terms of employment.

TIPS: If you're not using the Internet in your job search, it's time you moved into the 21st century. You need to be Internet literate if you want to find a good job and advance your career. You can get free Internet access through your local library or Americam Job Center. To locate the American Job Center closest to you, visit the following website or ask someone at your local library to access the site for you: jobcenter.usa.gov. You basically need to learn to do four things on the Internet related to your job search:

- Post your resume online to both general and specialty employment websites as well as to employer websites.
- Learn how to communicate by email, including how to submit your resume to online employment databases and send your resume to prospective employers and recruiters.
- Conduct research on various jobs and employers by using various search engines.
- Survey and respond to online job postings.

The sooner you begin incorporating the Internet in your job search, the more productive you should become in uncovering job lead and contacting prospective employers.

BARRIER #60
Rely too much on the Internet

QUESTIONS: Do you spend a great deal of time looking for jobs on the Internet? Are most of your job search Internet activities focused on posting your resume online and responding to job postings? Do you believe your next job may come via the Internet?

IF YES: While the Internet is an important job search tool, many job seekers become seduced by it and thus waste a great deal of time looking for jobs on the Internet. It can be a huge distraction with little results to show for the time and effort spent on responding to job postings and entering resumes into online resume databases. In fact, if you are spending more than 30 percent of your job search time surfing the Internet for jobs, you are probably engaged in wishful thinking, similar to spending a great deal of time responding to classified newspaper ads. Research shows that less than 30 percent of all job seekers found their last job because of their online job search activities. Most jobs are found through personal contacts and word-of-mouth efforts.

TIPS: There's nothing magical about the Internet. Use it wisely by focusing on those online activities that can have the highest payoff. Survey job postings of employment websites and companies and post your resume to online databases, such as Monster.com, Careerbuilder.com, and Indeed.com, but don't become preoccupied with such low payoff activities. The chances of being called for an interview based on such activities is probably a little better than being struck by lightning!

Be especially careful what you put on the Internet about yourself, including any personal blogs, entries into social networks, and a web resume. Employers increasingly do background checks on candidates by searching for an online presence. You could be embarrassed by what they find about you!

Focus most of your online efforts on conducting research about jobs and employers, networking for information and referrals, and acquiring additional job search skills related to your resume, letters, self-assessment, research, networking, and interviewing. The Internet offers a wealth of useful information for those who know how to access and use it properly.

BARRIER #61
Have personal issues that could interfere with your work

QUESTIONS: Do you often think about your personal situation while at work? Do you make personal phone calls during work hours, use the Internet for personal business (text, send emails, shop online, plan activities), or discuss your family, friends, finances, illnesses, or mental health with co-workers and/or your boss? Do you have your own part-time business which you sometimes do during your full-time job? Do you gossip while at work? Do you have childcare, illness, or physical or mental health disability issues that interfere with your work?

IF YES: However difficult, it's very important that you separate your personal life from your professional or work life. Employers hire you to do a job for them – not to help you solve your personal problems, use their resources to conduct your own business, or entertain others in the workplace. Employers are not social experiments. Personal issues are distractions in the workplace – they steal the employer's time, interfere with the work of others, and lead to your own low productivity. If you have a part-time business, be sure to keep it separate from your full-time job. Individuals who get caught up with direct-sales businesses, such as Amway, often pester their co-workers in the process of prospecting for new sales leads.

If you have childcare, illness, or learning, physical, or mental health disability issues, take care of these outside your work hours. Don't expect your employer to work for you. Remember, you are being paid to do a job for someone else – their money in exchange for your talent. Doing personal business or dealing with personal issues during work hours usually indicates a lack of interest in a job and is disrespectful of your boss and co-workers. It indicates you should be looking for work elsewhere. If not, a workplace with zero tolerance for such behavior will soon show you the door.

TIPS: There is no excuse for stealing time from your employer. Despite numerous distractions that intrude upon today's workplace, you need to be focused on doing your job. If you are addicted to personal phone calls, texting, email, and gossip, you may need some form of therapy. Otherwise, simply stop doing personal business during work hours. No phone calls, no texting, no emailing, and no talking to others about personal matters other than a few light moments during breaks or as part of the social culture of your organization. If you have friends and relatives calling you during work hours, inform them that you cannot accept such calls or talk with them during working hours. If you have difficulty telling them to stop such behavior, tell them you would appreciate it if they would stop contacting you during work hours since responding to them could get you fired; your company has a strict policy of no personal business on company time! Ask them to either contact you before or after work or during your lunch hour. If you have co-workers who engage in a lot of personal business, including gossip, let them know that you have work to do: *"Sorry I can't talk about such matters during working hours. I'm sure we both have work to do."* If they persist, see your supervisor and ask him or her what you should do about this situation. Chances are they can help. At least they will know you are not the one creating or contributing to such low productivity moments.

BARRIER #62
Fail to do adequate research on jobs and employers

QUESTIONS: Do you know little about various jobs and employers in your community? Do you go to job interviews without knowing what the organization actually does? Have you ever asked an interviewer *"What do you do here?"* Do you feel unprepared to deal with interview questions related to the job? Do you wish you knew more about job responsibilities, working conditions, and compensation related to various jobs and employers?

IF YES: Many job seekers approach the job market with a resume in the hope that someone will hire them based on the content of their resume. They do little other than look for job postings, send a resume, and wait to be called for a job interview. And they primarily do three things in preparation for the job interview: find directions to the interview location, pack a copy of their resume, and dress nicely for the encounter. Some even ask the killer question, *"What do you do here?"*

Such a red flag question clearly indicates the candidate was too lazy to learn anything about the organization. Not surprisingly, they are often unprepared to answer many questions relevant to the employer and they fail to ask good questions that indicate an interest in the company. If you don't conduct proper research, you will be entering the job market blindly, and you may be accepting a job which you will later discover was not the right one for you – if you are offered a job at all.

TIPS: There's no excuse for not doing some basic job and employer research. After all, most companies have a website describing what they do and the products and services they offer. If you are interested in a job with a particular organization, you should visit their website for employment information and/or contact the human resources office for information on the types of jobs offered within the organization. Many companies include an extensive and relatively sophisticated employment section on their home page that allows individuals to enter their resumes into a company database or apply online for specific positions. Indeed, companies are increasingly recruiting online for all types of positions, from entry-level to top management. Good examples come up when you search for jobs and careers at Cisco Systems (www.cisco.com), Google (www.google.com), Microsoft (https://careers.microsoft.com), and Boston Consulting Group (careers.bcg.com). You may be able to examine job postings which describe the duties and responsibilities of specific jobs as well as survey the profiles of key company personnel. Some companies even include information about the company culture and tips on conducting an effective job search with the company, including sample interview questions! Many of these business research websites are "must surfing" sites for job seekers. If you have only time to visit a few gateway business sites, make sure they include these seven:

- **CEO Express**   www.ceoexpress.com
- **Hoover's Online**   www.hoovers.com
- **Dun and Bradstreet's**
  Million Dollar Database   www.mergentmddi.com
- **Corporate Information**   www.corporateinformation.com
- **BizTech Network**   www.brint.com
- **Moodys**   www.moodys.com
- **Standard & Poors**   www.standardandpoors.com

If you are interested in working for federal, state, or local governments, each agency will have a personnel office which can supply you with descriptions of their jobs. To gain quick Internet access to **federal government** agencies, including vacancy announcements, go to the following websites:

- **FedWorld**   www.fedworld.gov
- **Federal Government Jobs**   federalgovernmentjobs.us
- **USA Jobs**   www.usajobs.gov

- **FederalJobsCentral**   www.fedjobs.com
- **Federal Jobs Digest**   www.jobsfed.com

Individuals oriented toward working in the **nonprofit sector** should visit these useful gateway websites:

- **GuideStar**   www.guidestar.org
- **Action Without Borders** www.idealist.org
- **Nonprofit Talent Match** nonprofittalentmatch.com
- **Encore**   encore.org
- **Common Good Careers**   commongoodcareers.org
- **Philanthropy**   www.philanthropy.com

As part of your research, you should explore various jobs and careers related to your interests and skills. One of the first places to start is the U.S. Department of Labor's bi-annual *Occupational Outlook Handbook* which is available in book form as well as online: www.bls.gov/ooh.

BARRIER #63
Appear desperate for a job

QUESTIONS: Are you desperate for a job? Are the tones of your cover letters and conversations that of someone in great need of a job? Do you try to convince employers that they should hire you because you really need the job? When you are asked, *"Why should I hire you?,"* is your answer very personal?

IF YES: Few employers are attracted to candidates who appear desperate for a job. Such individuals tend to be motivated by need and greed rather than by the nature of the work and their skills. People in great need may claim they can do anything, just to get the job. Once on the job, their performance will be less than stellar, and they may become burdens which employers do not wish to acquire. Desperate people tend to be very focused on making more money, because they have personal financial issues – most likely heavily indebted. Once hired, they may constantly pressure their boss for a raise because of personal needs rather than because of their on-the-job performance.

TIPS: Employers want to hire energetic and enthusiastic people they like and who can do the job well. If you are desperate for a job, try to quickly find a stop-gap job with a company that traditionally has a high turnover rate (construction, restaurants, real estate, retail sales, etc.) or contact a temporary employment firm. These are the proper employment arenas for individuals who need to take a break from other more permanent and career-oriented employment arenas. Once you get your personal life together, start looking for a more stable and career-oriented job that is both right for you and the employer.

Whatever you do, avoid talking about your personal situation in a job interview or on the job. Personal problems are red flags for employers. However sympathetic your boss and co-workers may be to your personal problems, such issues potentially impact negatively on the workplace. If you have serious personal problems, such as drug and alcohol addiction, and work for a large employer that has an Employee Assistance Program (EAP), by all means take advantage of this on-the-job service. It may be your last chance to get yourself together before you lose your job!

BARRIER #64
Primarily focus on salary and benefits

QUESTIONS: Are you primarily interested in salary and benefits when looking for a job? Do you include salary expectations on your resume? Do you plan to ask an employer about salary and benefits before you receive a job offer?

IF YES: Talking prematurely about money is a **big** red flag in a job search. Indeed, many job seekers make the mistake of asking about salary and benefits at the wrong time or prematurely revealing their salary expectations. If you want to quickly turn off an employer, ask about salary and benefits before being invited to an interview or early on in the job interview. When you ask about salary, employers make assumptions about your motivation – they assume you are primarily concerned with money rather than with doing the job. You appear needy and greedy rather than concerned about the needs of the employer and the requirements of the job. Once on the job, you will probably continue to focus on increasing your salary and benefits.

If you include salary expectations on your resume, you may be eliminated from further consideration because you are expecting too much money. Alternatively, you will be at a disadvantage in negotiating salary because you revealed your hand first. Indeed, the old poker saying that *"He who reveals his hand first loses the advantage"* is very relevant to the job search.

TIPS: Avoid talking about salary or revealing your salary expectations **before** being offered the job. If an interviewer asks about your salary expectations or salary requirements early in the interview, try to postpone your answer as well as turn the question around. For example, you might respond by saying, *"Before we talk about salary, I really need to know more about this job. By the way, what do you normally pay for someone with my qualifications?"* Always let the employer first indicate what he or she is willing to offer you – not what you are willing to accept. After all, you need to know what the job is worth by asking many questions about duties, responsibilities, and expected performance. Without that information, you simply don't know what the job is worth. Once you know what the employer is willing to pay, you will be in a stronger position to negotiate a salary that will be at the top of the employer's range. You also need to know what you are worth in today's job market, as well as in your community, before you negotiate salary and benefits.

Unfortunately, most job seekers don't know what they are worth in the job market, because they fail to do the necessary research on salary comparables. The good news is that several websites, such as <u>www.salary.com</u>, offer information on salary ranges for hundreds of jobs. In addition, your state employment office keeps current salary information on hundreds of jobs in or near your community (contact them or your local library). Before interviewing for a job, you should know what you are worth in today's job market. Once the employer reveals his or her compensation hand and you have a clear understanding of what the job is worth, you will be in a stronger position to negotiate a good salary.

I examine these and many other compensation issues, including negotiation scenarios, in three books: ***Give Me More Money!***, ***Get a Raise in 7 Days***, and ***Salary Negotiation Tips for Professionals***.

BARRIER #65
Try to fool employers

QUESTIONS: Do you think employers can be fooled? Have you included some falsehoods or stretched the truth on your resume? Do you make promises you most likely will not keep? Do you think many employers are naive when it comes to making personnel decisions? Are you a person of questionable character?

IF YES: Research shows that nearly 70 percent of all resumes include some falsehoods, from outright lies to embellishing the truth beyond what is considered acceptable. Many job seekers are tempted to hype their backgrounds with exaggerated statements about their experience and performance, or they omit important facts about themselves. Some simply lie on their resumes or during job interviews about their education and work experience. Many candidates assume employers will not investigate their background. Others feel they can manipulate employers into giving them a job. A few even assume employers are basically stupid. An occasional sociopath, who lies, manipulates, and steals on the job, gets hired. Character becomes a big issue with many employers, who are looking to hire individuals who are known for their honesty, integrity, loyalty, responsibility, tolerance, trustworthiness, and respect.

TIPS: If you lie or "stretch the truth" on your resume or during the interview, chances are this is a behavioral pattern that you will bring to the job. Indeed, it won't take long before an employer and co-workers discover who you really are – not the person represented on the resume or presented during job interviews. After a while, you will be seen for what you are – a deceptive and manipulative individual who does not tell the truth and who cannot be trusted. Your lies will become readily apparent, especially when it comes time to do the work. You'll be caught making excuses, exaggerating your performance, hiding your personal agenda, and stealing the employer's time during working hours. One thing is certain: once you lose trust and credibility, it won't be long before you lose your job. You'll be under close scrutiny as your supervisors begin documenting your failures to perform according to expectation.

You should be honest in what you say and do. If you lack expected education and training, don't try to make up for it by lying about your educational background. If you say you improved productivity by 50 percent in your last job, you may be asked to provide evidence of your claim or your productivity may be questioned in a reference check with your previous employer. If you keyboard 30 words a minute, don't state on your resume that you do 80 words minute – you may soon be tested and your lie discovered. Tell the positive side of your story – provide **evidence** that you can do the job. If you were fired from a previous job, it's not necessary to lie about what happened to you, nor do you have to volunteer this information.

If asked about why you left that particular job, tell your story in as positive terms as possible. Don't badmouth or blame others or show your anger about the situation. Take responsibility for what happened, however unfair, and focus on the future with this employer. What is important is what you have subsequently done, since employers are looking for **patterns of performance**. They obviously do not want to inherit a pattern that leads to firing you! Your experience is nothing new. You and millions of other people, perhaps including the person interviewing you, have been fired at sometime during their work life. Perhaps you made a mistake, but you learned from that experience and here is what you have accomplished since then. Again, tell a positive but truthful story.

Employers are not stupid. They know hiring is a risky and expensive business. They look for cues that tell them why they should and should not hire you. They increasingly do background checks that can quickly give them information on everything from your employment to your credit and criminal history. In today's high-tech world, there's no place to hide! Tell the truth and get on with a more rewarding and fulfilling life based upon **trust** and **achievements**.

BARRIER #66
Reveal a criminal history

QUESTIONS: Do you have a criminal history? Have you ever been arrested and convicted for DWI? Have you attempted to lie about your record? Are you currently on probation or parole? Have you recently been released from prison or jail?

IF YES: You're not alone. Over 2 million Americans are currently incarcerated in state and federal prisons. Between 10 and 11 million Americans circulate in and out of jails and detention centers each year. Nearly 700,000 people are released from state and local prisons each year. Over 5 million people are currently on probation or parole. And 77 million Americans have an arrest record. Over 70 percent of all incarcerated individuals are doing time for drug- and alcohol-related offenses or minor nonviolent crimes. Within three years nearly 70 percent of ex-offenders return to prison or jail.

Needless to say, millions of Americans have a criminal history that serves as a big red flag to employers who prefer not hiring such people. The good news is that many people with a record go on to find rewarding employment and satisfying careers with employers who are willing to give them a second chance. Many ex-offenders also start their own businesses and become successful entrepreneurs.

One of the first employment barriers many people with a record face is some version of the following dark question that appears on an application form or is asked during a job interview: *"Have you ever been arrested or convicted of a crime?"* If you answer *"Yes,"* chances are you may be immediately eliminated from further consideration since many employers discriminate against people with a criminal background. If you lie and say *"No,"* chances are your lie will be revealed during a background check or the truth will eventually surface once you are on the job – someone who knows about your background may show up and talk too much. While many states now "ban the box" (prohibit employers from asking this question on an application form), you still may need to address the question later in the job search, especially the during the job interview. If you lie when asked about your criminal activity, you may be setting yourself up for the day when you'll be fired for having lied to your employer.

At the same time, not all criminal activity is viewed equally by potential employers. There is a sliding scale of minor to very serious criminal behavior that can be threatening to a workplace. While many employers are willing to take a chance with someone who was convicted of a drug offense or some minor crime (college students, for example, are disproportionately arrested for public intoxication, disorderly conduct,

DUI, vandalism, and lewd public behavior), others are less willing to take a chance with someone who has embezzled funds, committed burglary, engaged in a violent crime, or was found guilty of a sex offense. Rapists, pedophiles, and murderers, for example, are especially avoided by employers because of their perceived habitual behavior, scary nature of their crimes, and high recidivism rates. If your criminal record includes these types of crimes, you may need special assistance related to therapy and medication that goes far beyond the scope of this and other recommended job search books.

TIPS: Soon-to-be-released and recently released ex-offenders face numerous barriers to re-entering the free world. While employment is one of their major barriers to getting on with their lives, housing, transportation, and health care pose additional barriers. Without a decent job, all these other "living basics" can come crashing down upon them and motivate them to once again engage in criminal activity in order to survive in the outside world.

If you are still incarcerated, you need to prepare yourself well for your re-entry transition. Start by working on your attitude and motivation and setting realistic goals. The following books will help you kick-start your new life:

- *7 Habits of Highly Effective People*
- *17 Lies That Are Holding You Back and the Truth That Will Set You Free*
- *100 Ways to Motivate Yourself*
- *Attitude Is Everything*
- *Awaken the Giant Within*
- *Change Your Attitude*
- *Finding Your Own North Star*
- *Goals!*
- *The Laws of Lifetime Growth*
- *The Power of Positive Thinking*
- *The Purpose-Driven Life*
- *The Success Principles*

Always tell the truth but do so in a particular manner that strengthens your candidacy. When responding to the application question about your criminal background, either leave the answer blank or write *"Will discuss this at the interview."* Your goal here is to get the interview – not prematurely eliminate yourself from consideration. It's during the interview where you can explain the situation and, more importantly, let the employer know that you have changed your life. Assure him or her that you have learned from your "youthful indiscretions" or "mistakes."

Many individuals with a criminal background also are restricted from doing certain types of jobs, such as working in law enforcement, child-care, financial institutions, schools, food service, and government. You need to know about any legal restrictions pertaining to your employment before applying for jobs.

The most difficult problem facing job seekers is **rejections**. Many people get disheartened after a few rejections. As an ex-offender, you will encounter numerous rejections in your job search. Some rejections will be due to your criminal background, whereas others will be the normal part of any job search. It's important that you accept all rejections as part of a job search. The more rejections you encounter, the closer you will be getting to an acceptance. For example, for every 25 contacts you make, maybe one will turn into a job interview. If you quit prematurely – after only five rejections – you'll never get to the acceptance. Successful job seekers accept rejections as part of the process and keep going until they get accepted. Keep motivated and focused as well as persist in finding the right job for you.

I deal extensively with these and many other employability issues in these books designed specifically for ex-offenders:

- *99 Days to Re-Entry Success Journal*
- *Best Jobs for Ex-Offenders*
- *Best Resumes and Letters for Ex-Offenders*
- *The Ex-Offender's 30/30 Job Solution*
- *The Ex-Offender's Job Interview Guide*
- *The Ex-Offender's New Job Finding and Survival Guide*
- *The Ex-Offender's Quick Job Hunting Guide*
- *The Ex-Offender's Re-Entry Assistance Directory*
- *The Ex-Offender's Re-Entry Success Guide*
- *The Re-Entry Employment and Life Skills Pocket Guide*
- *The Re-Entry Personal Finance Pocket Guide*

- *The Re-Entry Start-Up Pocket Guide*
- *Re-Imagining Life on the Outside Pocket Guide*

You also should visit these two websites, which include numerous resources to assist ex-offenders with a variety of re-entry issues:

- www.exoffenderreentry.com
- www.hirenetwork.org

BARRIER #67
Lack adequate or reliable transportation

QUESTIONS: Do you lack transportation to get to various job sites? Are you unable to acquire a reliable car or use public transportation? Is public transportation inadequate where you live? Are you unable to afford the high costs of commuting to work? Do you sometimes show up for work late or call in sick because of car problems? Are you restricted from driving for legal or health reasons?

IF YES: Employers expect you to regularly show up for work on time. Finding your way to work and maintaining your vehicle is your problem and thus should not impact on the employer and follow workers. If you don't have a vehicle, you'll need to find some other form of transportation. If you have an unreliable car that sometimes prevents you from coming to work, you need to solve that problem so it doesn't happen again. Repeated car problems are not acceptable excuses for missing work. In fact, being unable to solve your transportation problem indicates a lack of personal responsibility and may become grounds for dismissal if you're unable to show up for work on time.

If you're restricted from driving because of a legal judgment relating to a DUI or DWI, you also may need to explain the situation to your employer. If it's a health-related issue, you'll also need to inform your employer.

TIPS: Except on rare occasions (an accident, emergency breakdown, or unexpected service issue), never let your employer know that you are unable to get to work on time because of transportation issues. If you don't have a car or are unable to drive, be sure you solve your transportation problem before accepting a job. Check out how well you are serviced by public transportation, understand the daily costs of commuting, and make sure your working hours coincide with available public transportation.

Also, be very careful in accepting any job that requires a lengthy, costly, and nasty commute (also see Barrier #122 on pages 198-199). An employer who knows you must commute more than 45 minutes each way to work daily may be concerned that you may not stay long, especially if you find a job closer to home. Be prepared to deal with this possible objection to hiring you. Explain why such a commute works well for you – perhaps you also take your spouse to work or drop off children to a daycare facility, which is near where you will work. A lengthy commute will quickly get tiring and affect your enthusiasm for doing the job. When looking for a job, keep in mind the importance of transportation issues. They usually don't surface until **after** you have accepted a job. Most people want to find a job that's no more than 30 minutes from home. If that's also your goal, be sure to check out the unconventional job search tips I outline with my co-author Neil McNulty in *The Quick 30/30 Job Solution: Smart Job Search Tips for Surviving Today's New Economy*.

BARRIER #68
Lack a stable address or permanent housing

QUESTIONS: Will an employer be suspicious about where you live? Do you lack a permanent address? Is your housing situation considered "transitional"? Did you put a P.O. Box number on your resume rather than a street address? Do you rent a room or apartment?

IF YES: Employers want to know where you live, and they prefer hiring individuals who have a stable address. They also prefer homeowners who are more likely to stay at their current location. If your address appears too far to commute, an employer may want to know your plans for relocation. If, for example, you live 200 miles from the employer, you may not be given serious consideration unless you explain where you plan to live if you are offered the job.

TIPS: Always include a complete street mailing address on your resume as well as indicate your location in your email messages. If your housing situation is transient – you are staying in a hotel, YMCA, homeless shelter, or with a friend – include a street address that doesn't raise questions about your temporary housing situation.

BARRIER #69
Engage in wishful thinking

QUESTIONS: Do you believe it won't take you much time to land a job? Do you think employers will want to offer you a top salary? Do you expect to be offered a job after your first interview?

IF YES: Many job seekers engage in a great deal of wishful thinking about the job search, employers, and the hiring process. Most think this process won't take long – maybe a week or two. They also think they have a great resume that will result in many invitations to job interviews. They also expect to do well in the interview and be offered a job at a top salary. Much of this thinking is delusional since the reality of a job search is quite different. Unless you are going after a low-paying job with a high turnover rate, expect to spend many weeks looking for a job. It usually takes from three to six months to find a new job. Also, expect to encounter numerous rejections. For every 50 resumes you send out, expect to receive one invitation to a job interview. For every resume you post online, don't expect to hear from any employers unless you have a very exotic or high-demand skill. And once you are interviewed for a job, expect to be interviewed several times by the same employer before being offered the job.

TIPS: Be realistic in approaching your job search. First, expect this process to take a long time and involve numerous rejections. Second, be sure to write a first-class resume that grabs the attention of employers. Third, when you do get invited to a job interview, expect to be interviewed several times before being offered the job. Fourth, expect to be paid what you are worth based upon your past performance and comparable salaries for similar positions in your area. For a complete look at the job search, including many myths and realities, see my *Change Your Job, Change Your Life* as well as Richard Nelson Bolles's *What Color is Your Parachute?*, and Martin Yate's *Knock 'Em Dead*.

BARRIER #70
Don't know what you want to do

QUESTIONS: Are you unsure what you want to do? Do you start your job search by writing your resume? Do you know what you don't want to do? Do you have difficulty explaining to employers why you want to work for them?

IF YES: Many job seekers don't know what they want to do. As a result, they often present a picture of uncertainty to employers. The uncertainty is clearly reflected in the type of resume they write – a traditional chronological resume that lacks an objective and summarizes their work history by employers, inclusive employment dates, and assigned duties and responsibilities. Not knowing what they do well and enjoy doing, they let the employer interpret their resume, hoping their chronology of experience will sufficiently impress the employer to invite them to a job interview.

TIPS: Employers are busy people who don't have time to "read between the lines" and guess what it is you are likely to do for them. Consequently, your resume should **clearly** communicate your major strengths. It should tell employers exactly what you want to do – state an employer-oriented objective – and showcase what it is you are likely to do for them – provide evidence of your accomplishments. Most important of all, it should tell your story – who you are, what it is you have done (your performance) and can do (your skills), and what you are likely to do for this employer in the future (your continuing pattern of performance).

One of the best ways to tell your story is to do a thorough assessment of your interests, skills, and abilities that results in identifying your motivated abilities and skills. Once you know these, you'll be able to formulate a powerful employer-oriented objective and reveal in your resume and letters as well as during the interview exactly what it is you can do for the employer based upon your past pattern of performance as evidenced in your many supporting achievements. I outline in detail this whole self-assessment process, including how to identify your abilities and skills, state an objective, and write performance-oriented experience sections on your resume in these two books: *I Want to Do Something Else, But I'm Not Sure What It Is* and *High Impact Resumes and Letters*.

Most career counselors recommend that you take one or all of the following **assessments**: *Myers-Briggs Type Indicator®*, *The Self-Directed Search*, and *Strong Interest Inventory®*. You also may want to explore several websites that can help you assess your skills and abilities. Some tests are self-scoring and free of charge while others require interacting with a fee-based certified career counselor or testing expert. SkillsOne (www.skillsone.com), for example, is operated by the producers of the *Myers-Briggs Type Indicator®* and *Strong Interest Inventory®* – Consulting Psychologists Press (www.cpp.com). CareerLab (www.careerlab.com) offers one of the largest batteries of well respected assessment tools: *Campbell Interest and Skills Survey, Strong Interest Inventory®, Myers-Briggs Type Indicator®, 16-Personality Factors Profile, FIRO-B®, California Psychological Inventory (CPI), The Birkman Method,* and *Campbell Leadership Index.* The following websites are well worth exploring for both free and fee-based online assessments tools:

- **SkillsOne**   www.skillsone.com
  (Consulting Psychologists Press) www.cpp.com
- **CareerLab.com**   www.careerlab.com
- **Self-Directed Search®**   www.self-directed-search.com
- **Personality Online**   www.personalityonline.com
- **Keirsey Character Sorter**   www.keirsey.com
- **MAPP™**   www.assessment.com
- **Personality Type**   www.personalitytype.com

These 15 additional sites also include a wealth of related assessment devices that you can access online:

- **Analyze My Career**   www.analyzemycareer.com
- **Birkman Method**   www.birkman.com
- **Career Key**   www.careerkey.org/english
- **CareerLeader™**   www.careerleader.com
- **CareerPlanner.com**   www.careerplanner.com
- **CareerPerfect.com**   www.careerperfect.com
- **Careers By Design®**   www.careers-by-design.com
- **College Board**   www.myroad.college
                             board.com
- **Enneagram**   www.ennea.com
- **Humanmetrics**   www.humanmetrics.com
- **Jackson Vocational
  Interest Inventory**   www.jvis.com
- **My Future**   www.myfuture.com

- **People Management SMD**   www.peoplemanagementsmd.org
- **Profiler**   www.profiler.com
- **QueenDom**   www.queendom.com

BARRIER #71
Believe you're worth a lot more than your current pay

QUESTIONS: Were you brought up to believe that you shouldn't talk about money to others, especially what other people make? Do you believe you are currently underpaid? Do you think you'll be paid a lot more on your next job? Do you need to do salary research in order to find out what you're really worth? Do you feel uneasy negotiating salary and benefits? Do you believe most salaries are set by the employer and thus you have little room to negotiate? Are you reluctant to talk about money to a potential employer or your boss?

IF YES: Many people are basically "salary dumb" because they were brought up to believe it's impolite to ask people what they make or how much they are worth. Consequently, they are often clueless about what others make – a conspiracy of silence – and they are reluctant to do salary research involving asking about other people's incomes.

Most people also believe they are underpaid, even though they have little evidence that they are being paid less than what they are worth. When it comes time to negotiate salary, they either accept what is initially offered or they try to negotiate unrealistic terms of employment. If they did some basic research, they would quickly know exactly what they are worth in today's job market and thus be in a stronger position to negotiate a fair salary. Without such information, their answer to the *"What are your salary requirements?"* question will most likely be too high or too low.

Except for entry-level positions, most salaries are negotiable. In fact, candidates can often negotiate a salary that is 10 to 20 percent higher than the initial offer. But they need to know how best to negotiate salary. Unfortunately, many candidates make several of these negotiation mistakes:

1. Engaging in wishful thinking – believing you are worth a lot more than you are currently being paid but having no credible evidence of what you really should be paid.

2. Approaching the job search as an exercise in being clever and manipulative rather than being clear, correct, and competent in communicating your value to others.

3. Failing to research salary options and comparables and thus having few supports to justify your worth.

4. Failing to compile a list of specific accomplishments, including anecdotal one- to three-minute performance stories, that provide evidence of your value to employers.

5. Revealing salary expectations on the resume or in a letter.

6. Answers the question *"What are your salary requirements?"* before being offered the job.

7. Raising the salary question rather than waiting for the employer to do so.

8. Failing to ask questions about the company, job, and previous occupants of the position.

9. Asking *"Is this offer negotiable?"*

10. Quickly accepting the first offer, believing that's what the position is really worth and that an employer might be offended if one tries to negotiate.

11. Accepting the offer on the spot.

12. Accepting the offer primarily because of compensation.

13. Trying to negotiate compensation during the first interview.

14. Forgetting to consider the value of benefits and thus only focusing on the gross salary figure.

15. Focusing on benefits, stock options, and perks rather than on the gross salary figure.

16. Negotiating a salary figure rather discussing a salary range.

17. Negotiating over the telephone or by email.

18. Talking too much and listening too little.

19. Focusing on your needs rather than the employer's needs.

20. Trying to play "hardball."

21. Expressing a negative attitude toward the employer's offer.

TIPS: Be prepared to negotiate salary and benefits based upon your knowledge of compensation. Know what you are worth in today's job market by doing some basic salary research on salary comparables. For assistance with salary information and negotiations, be sure to visit these websites:

- **Salary.com**   www.salary.com
- **Quintessential Careers**   www.quintcareers.com/salary_ negotiation.html
- **Riley Guide**   www.rileyguide.com/salguides.html
- **JobStar**   jobstar.org/tools/salary/index.php
- **PayScale**   www.payscale.com/salary- negotiation-guide
- **Monster.com**   career-advice.monster.com
- **Jack Chapman**   salarynegotiations.com
- **SalaryExpert**   www.salaryexpert.com
- **Robert Half**   www.roberthalf.com

If you don't know how to negotiate compensation, you are well advised to learn some basic negotiation skills by consulting these books:

- *101 Salary Secrets*
- *Get a Raise in 7 Days: 10 Salary Steps to Success*
- *Give Me More Money!*
- *Negotiate Your Job Offer*
- *Negotiating Your Salary*
- *Salary Negotiation Tips for Professionals*

These books outline various steps for calculating your worth and conducting face-to-face negotiations, and include numerous sample dialogues.

BARRIER #72
Afraid to make a job or career change

QUESTIONS: Do you want to do something else but you're afraid to change jobs and careers? Do you avoid taking risks related to your career? Does the thought of quitting your job scare you? Do you feel locked into your current job?

IF YES: Jobs should not become life sentences. You should have the freedom to make job and career changes whenever necessary. Regardless of how much money you make, if you hate your job, you'll soon dislike yourself and others around you. Your life may become miserable and you'll probably go through bouts of depression. You'll grow much older than your actual age.

There's a lot more to life than money and a lousy job. As you've probably already discovered, money cannot bring you happiness – only financial security and larger toys. Unfortunately, millions of Americans are experiencing "job lock" – they are locked into jobs they dislike because of the salary and benefits. If they quit their jobs, they are afraid of losing their financial security, and they are not sure if they will be able to find another job with comparable salary and benefits.

At the same time, many people are starting new careers in their 50s and 60s related to their lifestyle goals. They are taking new risks that lead to career renewal accompanied by greater happiness and fulfillment.

TIPS: If you're unhappy with your current job, try to see if there is something you can do to restructure your job or move to another position in your company that would be a better fit for your interests, skills, and motivations. If that's not possible, start developing an action plan for a well organized job search that follows our 10-step process. For details on how you can best make a satisfying job or career change, see my *Change Your Job, Change Your Life*.

BARRIER #73
Apply for jobs unrelated to your qualifications

QUESTIONS: Do you sometimes apply for jobs that don't really relate to your background and experience? Do you try to fit into jobs rather than find jobs fit for you? Do you send out lots of resumes for many different types of jobs?

IF YES: It's easy for employers to eliminate 90 percent of the resumes they receive because most candidates are not qualified for the advertised position. In fact, employers are often surprised that so many unqualified candidates waste their time applying for a position they know they are not qualified for. Don't engage in wishful thinking, or think you are making progress with your job search, by applying for such positions.

TIPS: When applying for a job, read the qualifications carefully. If you meet the minimum requirements and you think it would be a job you would do well and enjoy doing, by all means apply for it. But if you lack the necessary qualifications, don't engage in wishful thinking and waste your time applying for the position.

BARRIER #74
Show a history of job hopping

QUESTIONS: Have you held more than two jobs during the past five years? Are you always looking for another job? Do you soon get bored with a new job? Do you include the exact month and year of employment dates for each job you held? Do you have difficulty explaining why you have held so many jobs?

IF YES: As we noted in Tip #10 (see page 26), job hoppers are costly hires. If you are a job hopper, you can do certain things to minimize your checkered employment record and, hopefully, begin developing a new pattern of stable employment.

Many job seekers have a clear history of job hopping which they inadvertently accentuate on their resumes by including a chronology of experience by date and month. For example, if you were an employer reviewing a resume that included this chronology of employment, what might you conclude about the candidate?

- March 2015 to July 2015
- January 2014 to November 2014
- February 2013 to October 2013
- July 2012 to December 2012
- April 2012 to February 2013

If you are like most employers, you would conclude that this candidate can't keep a job for long. Since he has a clear history of job hopping, you would waste your time interviewing and hiring such a person. And you're really not interested in learning why he changed jobs so frequently – fired, laid off, quit. You see an employment pattern you don't want to inherit. The only exception would be in the case of a student who held several part-time jobs while attending college. In that case, this pattern is understandable and excusable.

TIPS: If you are an obvious job hopper, you need to do three things. First, don't accentuate your poor pattern of employment by using a chronological resume that includes both months and years. Use a functional resume that stresses your common skills. Second, try to keep a job for at least three years so you can start breaking this pattern. If an employer knows you are a job hopper, she would be foolish to invest much time and money training you for a future with the company. After all, she will probably be training you for your next job with another employer! Third, if you're not planning to break your job hopping pattern, look for jobs with a high turnover rate, such as in construction, farming, food service, retail sales, and cleaning services. However, don't expect to make much money on these jobs since many high-turnover jobs also are low-paying, part-time jobs with limited benefits.

BARRIER #75
Unable to pass employment screening tests

QUESTIONS: Do you have difficulty passing tests? Are you likely to fail a drug trust? Do you lack the temperament to do some jobs? If you are tested against the claims you make on your resume, might you have a problem demonstrating your capabilities?

IF YES: Many employers require a variety of pre-employment tests. These might include drug testing, psychological profiles, polygraph exams, skills tests, and on-the-job simulations. If, for example, you are subjected to a "situational interview," you will be asked to perform in a situation that approximates a real on-the-job situation, such as handling a customer service complaint. If you are being hired for a security-related position, you may need to take a polygraph exam. Employers hiring for sales positions may administer psychological tests that indicate how effective a salesperson you may be.

TIPS: Be prepared for pre-employment screening tests. If, for example, you claim you can keyboard 120 words a minute, make sure you can pass a test at the 120-word rate. If not, give a more accurate claim about your keyboarding skills. If you use drugs, you will have a problem with some employers who now require both pre-employment screening for drugs and random on-the-job drug testing. You simply need to quit drugs if you hope to pass drug tests. Don't expect to prepare for most screening tests. Just be aware that you may have to take tests that will review who you really are, especially what motivates you and what you do well.

BARRIER #76
Unlikely to get a positive background check

QUESTIONS: Do you have any red flags in your background that might be revealed through a background check? Have you had problems with previous employers who might tell a prospective employer that you may not be a good employee? Have you neglected to reconcile with previous employers with whom you had a negative relationship?

IF YES: More and more employers conduct thorough background checks on potential employees. They look for any red flags that would give them cause not to hire you. A background check can reveal that you have a criminal record, declared bankruptcy, collected Workers' Compensation, sued a previous employer, are disliked by co-workers or neighbors, or have health problems or an addiction. Your references may not give you a positive recommendation.

TIPS: Do a background check on yourself **before** you let a prospective employer check you out. You may be using the same source as an employer – an online background checker who charges anywhere from $29.00 to $99.00 to do a basic background check, which may include credit information. If you have a bad relationship with a previous employer, try to neutralize that relationship by letting them know what you are now doing and informing them that they may be contacted soon as part of a routine background check. Regardless of how bad your relationship may have been, most employers will wish you well and basically verify your employment dates with them. Few will say anything negative about you. After all, they could be sued by an ex-employee who did not get a job because of their negative evaluation. Be sure to let your references know you are conducting a job search, and share with them your resume and the type of job you are seeking. The more information they have about you, the more positive things they may be able to say about you. You don't want a prospective employer to contact one of the references who says, *"Oh, I didn't know she was looking for a job. What is she interested in doing now?"*

BARRIER #77
Reveal a history of on-the-job injuries and Workers' Compensation claims

QUESTIONS: Have you ever been injured on the job? Did you put in a Workers' Compensation claim for your injuries? Have you done this more than once during the past 10 years?

IF YES: While most employers are required to carry Workers' Compensation insurance, they also are concerned about hiring individuals who have a history of getting injured on the job and collecting Workers' Compensation. Indeed, many employees put in fraudulent claims which, in turn, drive up employer's insurance costs and lower their productivity.

TIPS: If you are injury-prone and have a history of making Workers' Compensation claims, you should seriously consider pursuing some other line of work that is much safer. Employers don't need high-cost employees who are often out of work and making insurance claims against the company.

BARRIER #78
Running a business while looking for a job

QUESTIONS: Do you own a business? Are you involved in a part-time business that could distract from your full-time job? Did you include your personal business involvement on your resume?

IF YES: While many employers admire entrepreneurial employees, they may be reluctant to hire someone who also has a business on the side. Such involvement raises questions about your long-term commitment to the employer. If you include your business on your resume, you may send a prospective employer a mixed message – you're not sure who you really want to work for, yourself or the employer who's reading your resume. Chances are your personal business will interfere with their regular job. Employers want your entrepreneurial spirit directed to their company.

TIPS: If you are involved in some type of direct-sales business (Amway, Shaklee, Avon, Mary Kay, Herbalife) that requires you to regularly prospect for new clients among friends and colleagues, do not bring that business into the workplace. Doing so can be disruptive and intimidating. That is something you should only do outside your regular job. Be very careful about involving your co-workers in such a business. They may not appreciate being pestered by salespeople, especially ones they have to work with regularly!

If you are only looking for a stop-gap job to support yourself while building your own business, be truthful with prospective employers who may be concerned about how long you will stay with them. If you are looking for a job after failing at your own business, be prepared to assure the employer that you are serious about working for someone else rather than trying to get your feet back on the ground to re-grow your business. The problem with entrepreneurs is that they tend to be very self-centered rather than employer-centered. If you have a habit of always talking about your latest get-rich-quick scheme, kill it at work. No one wants to keep hearing about your latest illusions or delusions.

7

Networks, Applications, Resumes, and Letters

"Make sure you hone your interpersonal and writing skills to clearly communicate your qualifications to employers."

BARRIER #79
Fail to network for information, advice, and referrals

QUESTIONS: Do you have difficulty making cold calls? Do you prefer not having to introduce yourself to strangers? Are you more comfortable sending resumes and letters in response to job postings than picking up the telephone to contact someone about a job?

IF YES: All things being equal, employers prefer hiring people they know or hiring someone referred to them by someone they trust. Networking is the key to finding jobs on the hidden job market. It's the process of acquiring information, advice, and referrals through people. Effective networkers know how to quickly connect with other people as well as build and nurture relationships for the purpose of finding a job.

Many people acknowledge the importance of networking in their job search as well as on the job. They understand how it works, but they have difficulty actually doing it. Your mother's old admonishment that *"You shouldn't talk to strangers"* is in part responsible for this reluctance to network. As a result, many shy and introverted job seekers sit on the sidelines content with primarily looking for jobs on the advertised job market.

Within the context of the job search, networking involves a purposeful process of connecting, building, and nurturing relationships in order to acquire information, advice, and referrals. Test your networking I.Q. by responding to each of the following statements:

Are You a Savvy Networker?

INSTRUCTIONS: Respond to each statement by circling the number to the right that best represents your situation. The higher your score, the higher your "Savvy Networking IQ."

SCALE: 1 = Strongly agree   4 = Disagree
            2 = Agree   5 = Strongly disagree
            3 = Maybe, not certain

1. I enjoy going to business and social functions where I have an opportunity to meet new people. (CONNECT/BUILD)   5 4 3 2 1

2. I usually take the initiative in introducing myself to people I don't know. (CONNECT)   5 4 3 2 1

3. I enjoy being in groups and actively participating in group activities. (CONNECT/BUILD)   5 4 3 2 1

4. On a scale of 1 to 10, my social skills are at least a "9." (BUILD/NURTURE)   5 4 3 2 1

5. I listen carefully and give positive feedback when someone is speaking to me. (CONNECT/BUILD)   5 4 3 2 1

6. I have a friendly and engaging personality that attracts others to me. (CONNECT/BUILD/ NURTURE)   5 4 3 2 1

7. I make a special effort to remember people's names and frequently address them by their name. (CONNECT)   5 4 3 2 1

8. I carry business cards and often give them to acquaintances from whom I also collect business cards. (CONNECT)   5 4 3 2 1

9. I have a system for organizing business cards I receive, including notes on the back of each card. (BUILD)   5 4 3 2 1

10. I seldom have a problem starting a conversation and engaging in small talk with strangers. (CONNECT)   5 4 3 2 1

11. I enjoy making cold calls and persuading strangers to meet with me. (CONNECT)   5 4 3 2 1

12. I usually return phone calls in a timely manner. (CONNECT)   5 4 3 2 1

13. If I can't get through to someone on the phone, I'll keep trying until I do, even if it means making 10 more calls. (CONNECT)   5 4 3 2 1

14. I follow up on new contacts by phone, email, or letter. (BUILD)   5 4 3 2 1

15. I have several friends who will give me job leads. (BUILD)   5 4 3 2 1

16. I frequently give and receive referrals. (BUILD)   5 4 3 2 1

17. I have many friends. (BUILD)   5 4 3 2 1

18. I know at least 25 people who can give me career advice and referrals. (BUILD)   5 4 3 2 1

19. I don't mind approaching people with my professional concerns. (CONNECT/BUILD)   5 4 3 2 1

20. I enjoy having others contribute to my success. (BUILD)   5 4 3 2 1

21. When I have a problem or face a challenge, I usually contact someone for information and advice. (BUILD)   5 4 3 2 1

22. I'm good at asking questions and getting useful advice from others. (BUILD)   5 4 3 2 1

23. I usually handle rejections in stride by learning from them and moving on. (BUILD)   5 4 3 2 1

24. I can sketch a diagram, with appropriate linkages, of individuals who are most important in both my personal and professional networks. (BUILD)   5 4 3 2 1

25. I regularly do online networking by participating in various interest groups, newsgroups, mailing lists, chats, and bulletin boards. (CONNECT/BUILD)   5 4 3 2 1

26. I regularly communicate my accomplishments to
    key members of my network. (NURTURE)   5 4 3 2 1

27. I make it a habit to stay in touch with members
    of my network by telephone, email, Facetime,
    Skype, and letter. (NURTURE)   5 4 3 2 1

28. I regularly send personal notes, birthday and
    holiday greeting cards, and letters for special
    occasions to people in my network. (NURTURE)   5 4 3 2 1

29. I still stay in touch with childhood friends and
    former classmates. (NURTURE)   5 4 3 2 1

30. I have a great network of individuals whom I can
    call on at anytime for assistance, and they will be
    happy to help me. (BUILD/NURTURE)   5 4 3 2 1

31. I belong to several organizations, including a
    professional association. (CONNECT/BUILD)   5 4 3 2 1

32. I consider myself an effective networker who
    never abuses my relationships. (CONNECT/
    BUILD/NURTURE)   5 4 3 2 1

33. Others see me as a savvy networker.
    (CONNECT/BUILD/NURTURE)   5 4 3 2 1

TOTAL I.Q. [   ]

If your total composite I.Q. is above 155, you're most likely a savvy networker. If you're below 120, you're probably lacking key networking skills. Each of the above items indicates a particular **connect, build,** or **nurture** behavior or skill that contributes to one's overall networking effectiveness. Concentrate on improving those skills on which you appear to be weak. For example, you may discover you are particularly savvy at "connecting" with people but you're weak on "building" and "nurturing" relationships – or vice versa – that define your network.

TIPS: Numerous books can assist you in developing effective networking skills. I previously identified several key networking books in my discussion of Barrier #28 – Shy and Introverted. If you're new to both interpersonal and electronic networking, I also recommend that you consult the following resources, which are available through Impact Publications in print form (see the order form at the end of this book):

- *Branding Yourself*
- *Guerrilla Marketing for Job Hunters*
- *How to Find a Job on LindedIn, Facebook, Twitter, and Google+*
- *Job Searching With Social Media for Dummies*
- *Knock 'Em Dead Social Networking*
- *LinkedIn for Dummies*
- *The Power Formula for LinkedIn Success*
- *Resumes for Dummies*
- *The Social Media Job Search Workbook*

You should be able to find eBook versions of most of these resources for iBooks, Kindle, Nook, and other platforms on <u>Amazon.com</u>, <u>barnes andnoble.com</u>, and <u>iTunes</u>.

At the same time, networking is increasingly taking on new communication forms in today's high-tech world. Job seekers can take advantage of several websites and electronic databases for conducting a job search, from gathering information on the job market to disseminating resumes to employers. The Internet also allows job seekers to network for information, advice, and job leads. You can use social media, blogs, chat groups, message boards, and email to gather job information and make contacts with potential employers. Using email, you can make personal contacts which give you job leads for further networking via computer or through the more traditional networking methods outlined in this chapter.

Several websites will help you develop networking skills as well as put you in contact with important employment-related networks. These three websites include a wealth of information on the networking process and serve as useful gateway networking sites for job seekers:

- **Quintessential Careers**   <u>www.quintcareers.com/ networking.html</u>
- **Riley Guide**   <u>www.rileyguide.com/netintv.html</u>
- **My Career Transition**s   <u>mycareertransitions.com</u>

Once you begin the process of developing your networks, you may want to use the following websites to locate long-lost friends, classmates, and others who might be helpful in your networking campaign:

- **AnyWho**   www.anywho.com
- **Classmates**   www.classmates.com
- **Reunion** (high school)   www.reunion.com
- **Switchboard**   www.switchboard.com
- **Yahoo! People Search**   search.yahoo.com

If you wish to locate some of your former military buddies, be sure to explore these people finders for locating military personnel:

- **Buddy Finder**   www.military.com/BuddyFinder
- **GI Search.com**   www.gisearch.com
- **Military Locator**   www.militarylocator.com
- **VetFriends**   www.vetfriends.com

If you've lost contact with your former classmates, try these websites for locating alumni groups:

- **Alumni.net**   www.alumni.net
- **Curious Cat Alumni
  Connections**   www.curiouscat.net/alumni

The popular trend or fad in online networking is based upon the "six degrees of separation theory" – everyone is connected to everyone else in the world by only six other people. Building electronic communities, these networks are designed to put users into contact with thousands of other people for all types of purposes – from dating to making friends to finding a job to recruiting to developing sales forces to closing business deals. These electronic networks offer some interesting online networking opportunities for those who have the time and dedication to make them work. They probably are most effective for those who need to prospect for new business and potential sales contacts, which is the direction many of the more entrepreneurial such networks now take.

Opportunities to do online networking relating to jobs and careers are numerous. The three major social networking groups enable users to profile themselves online and make connections:

- **LinkedIn**   www.linkedin.com
- **Facebook**   www.facebook.com
- **Twitter**   www.twitter.com

LinkedIn is by far the most widely used for professional branding and job search. You are well advised to incorporate LinkedIn in your job search. You'll find a great deal of information on the Internet about how to best use LinkedIn for finding employment.

Other up-and-coming networking groups include:

- **Tumbir**   www.tumbir.com
- **Ryze**   www.ryze.com
- **Ning**   www.ning.com
- **Groupsite**   www.groupsite.com
- **Pinterest**   www.pinterest.com
- **Meetup**   www.meetup.com
- **Networking for Professionals**   networkingforprofessionals.com

The Internet can thus significantly enhance your job search. It offers new networking possibilities for individuals who are literate in today's digital technology. Be sure get your resume into various employment websites. Explore their job postings, resources, chat groups, and message boards. Within just a few minutes of electronic networking, you may pick up important job information, advice, and leads that could turn into a real job.

BARRIER #80
Use the wrong networking approach

QUESTIONS: Do you believe networking primarily involves attending business meetings and social hours where individuals meet strangers by passing out business cards? Are you uncertain how to network for job-related information, advice, and referrals? Do you make a new contact but fail to follow up? Do you try to ask for advice with the idea of trying to get a job with the person you've contacted for advice?

IF YES: Many job seekers commit a variety of networking errors that all but terminate an otherwise useful networking campaign. Avoid doing the following:

1. Fail to develop and sustain a well organized and targeted campaign for building, expanding, and nurturing one's network of relationships.

2. Become a networking pest, similar to direct-sales people who are constantly in one's face trying to sell products.

3. Contact the wrong people or engage in networking activities with losers who have very little to offer a job seeker.

4. Confuse networking with taking advantage of people.

5. Turn off potential networking contacts by asking them for a job rather than for information, advice, and referrals.

6. Lie about one's true intentions in making a contact and asking for referrals.

7. Exploit relationships for personal gain rather than for mutual support.

8. Fail to express one's gratitude for the contact's time and assistance.

9. Abuse a contact's time and relationships.

10. Believe one must be aggressive and obnoxious rather than pleasant, persistent, and professional when networking.

TIPS: Effective networkers understand how to network properly. They do not use other people for the purpose of getting a job. They don't make pests of themselves. Their purpose is to penetrate the hidden job market where they can acquire information, advice, and referrals related to their employment interests. Throughout this process, you must be honest with what you are doing. Never ask a contact for a job. Always ask for **information, advice, and referrals**. When you ask someone for a job, you put them on the spot and make them feel uncomfortable; they don't want to become responsible for your employment fate. But when you ask people for information, advice, and referrals, including complete strangers, you will be surprised how helpful individuals will be. In fact, the best way to get a job is to ask individuals within your growing network for information, advice, and referrals.

BARRIER #81
Unwilling to take the necessary actions

QUESTIONS: Do you understand how to get a job but find it difficult to actually land a job? Do you often get discouraged after being rejected for a possible opportunity? Do you have difficulty finding enough time to conduct your job search? Are you spending less than two hours a day on your job search?

IF YES: You must keep focused, motivated, and committed throughout your job search. It's not surprising that the single most important impediment to conducting a successful job search is the **failure to implement**. While you can have all the dreams, plans, and positive thinking you want, if you don't translate those dreams, plans, and thinking into daily and weekly plans of action, you will be going nowhere with your job search. In fact, it's no surprise to discover that many job seekers actually spend little time on their job search. They talk about it, lament the fact that no one calls them, send out a few resumes and letters in response to job postings, and wait to be contacted by potential employers for job interviews.

TIPS: Effective job seekers tend to be very **proactive**. They **routinize** several job search activities, especially research and networking, and target employers they believe would be a perfect fit for their interests, skills, and motivations. They understand the importance of **implementation**, which involves translating their ideas and goals into specific action steps.

One of the best ways to jump-start your job search is to commit yourself in writing by completing the **Job Search Contract** and **Weekly Job Performance and Planning Report** on pages 131 and 132. This contract and report will serve as key documents for both prioritizing and implementing your job search as well as keeping you focused and motivated on what you need to do in order to conduct a successful job search.

BARRIER #82
Fail to properly complete applications

QUESTIONS: Do you avoid answering some application questions? Are you afraid of making spelling and grammatical errors? Do you arrive at a job site unprepared to provide all the information asked for on an application?

IF YES: Just like a resume or letter, it's important that you complete an error-free application. After all, your application is a calling card for a job information and a possible job offer. It should represent your best effort. If you make spelling and grammatical errors, you will make a bad impression on a potential employer. If you fail to respond to each

Job Search Contract

1. I'm committed to changing my life by changing my job.

   Today's date is_____.

2. I will manage my time so that I can successfully complete my job search and find a high quality job. I will begin changing my time management behavior on_____.

3. I will begin my job search on_____.

4. I will involve_____with my job search.
   (individual/group)

5. I will spend at least one week conducting research on different jobs, employers, and organizations. I will begin this research during the week of _____.

6. I will complete my skills identification step by _____.

7. I will complete my objective statement by _____.

8. I will complete my resume by _____.

9. Each week I will:

   - make_____new job contacts.

   - conduct_____informational interviews.

   - follow up on_____referrals.

10. My first job interview will take place during the week of_____.

11. I will begin my new job by_____.

12. I will make a habit of learning one new skill each year.

Signature: _____

Date: _____

Weekly Job Performance and Planning Report

1. The week of: _____.

2. This week I:

   - wrote_____job search letters.
   - sent_____resumes and_____letters to potential employers.
   - completed_____applications.
   - made_____job search telephone calls.
   - completed_____hours of job research.
   - set up_____appointments for informational interviews.
   - conducted_____informational interviews.
   - received_____invitations to a job interview.
   - followed up on_____contacts and_____referrals.

3. Next week I will:

   - write_____job search letters.
   - send_____resumes and_____letters to potential employers.
   - complete_____applications.
   - make_____job search telephone calls.
   - complete_____hours of job research.
   - set up_____appointments for informational interviews.
   - conduct_____informational interviews.
   - follow up on_____contacts and_____referrals.

4. Summary of progress this week in reference to my Job Search Contract commitments: _____

   _____

   _____

   _____

   _____

   _____

   _____

question, you will appear to be unprepared or trying to hide something. If asked to list your references and you have none to list, or can't recall their contact information, you look unprepared.

TIPS: Be prepared to complete an error-free application. Effective writers of job applications do the following:

1. Prepare to complete each section of a job application by bringing all the necessary information needed to the application site, including salary history and lists of previous employers and references.
2. Answer all questions as completely as possible.
3. Select references carefully – only those who can give them a strong recommendation.
4. Handle sensitive red flag questions honestly and tactfully. If, for example, they are asked about being dismissed from previous jobs or convicted of a crime, they state "Will discuss at the interview" rather than leave these sections blank or just say "Yes."
5. Attach an achievement-oriented resume to the application if appropriate.
6. Ask about the selection process and hiring decision.
7. Follow up the application with a telephone call.

I outline these and several other application tips in *Resume, Application, and Letter Tips for People With Hot and Not-So-Hot Backgrounds*.

BARRIER #83
Don't write and send different types of powerful job search letters

QUESTIONS: Do you neglect to send thoughtful cover and thank-you letters to prospective employers? Do you find it difficult to compose letters that express your skills and personality? Are you uncertain what to include in a cover letter? Do you believe a resume is more important to getting a job than a letter?

IF YES: Many job seekers fail to include a thoughtful cover letter with their resume. When sending a letter by email, many people merely write: "See the attached resume" or "I'm sending my resume in response to your position." Furthermore, few job seekers send thank-you letters after a job interview. And ever fewer job seekers send approach letters. However, employers often report that it was the quality of a candidate's cover and thank-you letters, rather than their resume, that made the difference in the hiring process. Unlike a standard resume, job search letters allow you to express your personality, energy, and enthusiasm – important qualities that help define your **likability**.

TIPS: Cover letters, which accompany resumes, are only one of several types of letters you need to write during your job search. Other important job search letters include:

- Resume letters
- "T" letters
- Approach letters
- Thank-you letters

Some of the most powerful job search letters you can write are thank-you letters. These letters are usually remembered by employers because few candidates are thoughtful enough to send such letters. Different types of thank-you letters should be written on various job search occasions:

- Post-job interview
- After an informational interview
- Responding to a rejection
- Withdrawing from consideration
- Accepting a job offer
- Terminating employment

These are some of the most neglected yet most important written communications in any job search. If you write these letters, your job search may take you much further than you expected. Indeed, you may be surprised by the positive responses to your candidacy! Numerous examples of these types of job search letters can be found in several of my other job search books: *201 Dynamite Job Search Letters*, *High Impact Resumes and Letters*, *Nail the Cover Letter!* and *Best Resumes and Letters for Ex-Offenders*. Also, see Wendy S. Enelow's *Best Cover Letters for $100,000-+ Jobs* and Daniel Porot's and Frances Bolles Haynes's *Winning Letters That Overcome Barriers to Employment*.

BARRIER #84
Make numerous resume errors

QUESTIONS: Are you uncertain what should and should not go on a resume? Do you feel your resume could use some professional help? Does your resume primarily summarize your past work history? Did you have difficulty writing your resume, including an employer-oriented objective?

IF YES: What should or should not be included in a resume? What are some of the common mistakes job seekers make? Job seekers repeatedly make numerous resume errors that knock them out of competition. Make sure your resume is not dead upon arrival, by avoiding these frequently observed resume **writing errors**:

1. Unrelated to the position in question.
2. Too long or too short.
3. Unattractive with a poorly designed format, small type style, and crowded copy.
4. Misspellings, poor grammar, wordiness, and repetition.
5. Punctuation errors.
6. Lengthy phrases, long sentences, and awkward paragraphs.
7. Slick, amateurish, or "gimmicky" – appears over-produced.
8. Boastful, egocentric, and aggressive.
9. Dishonest, untrustworthy, or suspicious information.
10. Missing critical categories, such as experience, skills, and education.
11. Difficult to interpret because of poor organization and lack of focus – uncertain what the person has done or can do.
12. Unexplained time gaps between jobs.
13. Too many jobs in a short period of time – a job hopper with little evidence of career advancement.
14. No evidence of past accomplishments or a pattern of performance from which to predict future performance; primarily focuses on formal duties and responsibilities that came with previous jobs.
15. Lacks credibility and content – includes much fluff and canned resume language.

16. States a strange, unclear, or vague objective.
17. Appears over-qualified or under-qualified for the position.
18. Includes distracting personal information that does not enhance the resume nor the candidate.
19. Fails to include critical contact information (telephone number and email address) and uses an anonymous address (P.O. Box number).
20. Uses jargon and abbreviations unfamiliar to the reader.
21. Embellishes name with formal titles, middle names, and nicknames which make him or her appear odd or strange.
22. Repeatedly refers to "I" and appears self-centered.
23. Lacks keywords and key phrases for quick assessing or scanning the resume.
24. Ends with the rather empty statement "References available upon request." One would hope so!
25. Includes too much personal information or just too much information overall, which makes the reader uneasy and exhausted from trying to make some analytical sense of the document.
26. Includes obvious self-serving references that raise credibility questions.
27. Sloppy, with handwritten corrections – crosses out "married" and writes "single"!
28. Includes red flag information such as being incarcerated, fired, lawsuits or claims, health or performance problems, or stating salary figures, including salary requirements, that may be too high or too low.
29. Includes a very narrow, self-serving objective that turns off readers.
30. Too unconventional – needs to stay "inside the box."

Employers also report encountering several of these **production, distribution, and follow-up errors**:

1. Poorly typed and reproduced – hard to read.
2. Produced on odd-sized paper.
3. Too unconventional, such as using rainbow colors and perfumed paper.

4. Printed on poor quality paper or on extremely thin or thick paper.

5. Soiled with coffee stains, fingerprints, or ink marks.

6. Sent to the wrong person or department.

7. Mailed, faxed, or emailed to "To Whom It May Concern" or "Dear Sir."

8. Emailed as an attachment which could have a virus if opened.

9. Enclosed in a tiny envelope that requires the resume to be unfolded and flattened several times.

10. Arrived without proper postage – the employer gets to pay the extra!

11. Sent the resume by the slowest postage rate possible.

12. Envelope double-sealed with tape and is indestructible – nearly impossible to open by conventional means!

13. Back of envelope includes a handwritten note stating that something is missing on the resume, such as a telephone number, email address, or new mailing address.

14. Resume taped to the inside of the envelope, an old European habit practiced by paranoid letter writers. Need to destroy the envelope and perhaps also the resume to get it out of the envelope!

15. Accompanied by extraneous or inappropriate enclosures which were not requested, such as copies of self-serving letters or recommendations, transcripts, or samples of work.

16. Arrives too late for consideration.

17. Comes without a cover letter.

18. Cover letter repeats what was on the resume – does not command attention nor move the reader to action.

19. Sent the same or different versions of the resume to the same person as a seemingly clever follow-up method.

20. Follow-up call made too soon – before the resume and letter arrive!

21. Follow-up call is too aggressive or the candidate appears too "hungry" for the position – appeared needy or greedy.

TIPS: Since the resume is vitally important to getting a job interview, make sure your resume is error-free. Spend sufficient time crafting a resume that shouts loud and clear that you are someone who should be interviewed for a position. I examine how to write, produce, distribute, and follow-up error-free resumes in *Nail the Resume!*, *High Impact Resumes and Letters*, *The Savvy Resume Writer*, *Blue-Collar Resume and Job Hunting Guide*, *Best Resumes and Letters for Ex-Offenders*, *Best Resumes and CVs for International Jobs*, and *Resume, Application, and Letter Tips for People With Hot and Not-So-Hot Backgrounds*. If you have difficulty writing your own resume, contact a professional resume writer who can help you put together a first-class resume. Professional resume writers belong to the following organizations, which are good sources for shopping for such talent:

- **Professional Association of Resume Writers and Career Coaches**   www.parw.com
- **National Resume Writers' Association**   www.thenrwa.com
- **Career Directors International**   careerdirectors.com
- **International Coach Federation**   www.internationalcoach federation.com

You can see some terrific examples of their work by reviewing the following resume books written by professional resume writers, which are available in many libraries, online, or through Impact Publications (www.impactpublications.com):

- *101 Best Resumes*
- *Best KeyWords for Resumes, Cover Letters, and Interviews*
- *Best Resumes and Letters for Ex-Offenders*
- *Best Resumes for People Without a Four-Year Degree*
- *Expert Resumes for Manufacturing Careers*
- *Gallery of Best Resumes for People Without a Four-Year Degree*
- *High Impact Resumes and Letters*
- *Knock 'Em Dead Resume Templates*
- *Knock 'Em Dead Resumes*
- *Modernize Your Resume: Get Noticed . . . Get Hired*
- *The Resume Catalog*
- *Resume Magic*
- *Resumes for Dummies*

Indeed, you can learn a great deal about resumes for particular occupations by examining the many resume examples in these books.

For a new approach to resume writing, production, and distribution, check out LinkedIn's **free resume templates** for quickly turning a LinkedIn profile into a customized resume: resume.linkedinlabs.com

Many other job search websites also offer templates for creating an online resume.

- www.parw.com
- www.prwra.com
- www.cminstitute.com
- www.nrwaweb.com

BARRIER #85
Make numerous letter errors

QUESTIONS: Do you have difficulty writing letters that would persuade a prospective employer to interview you? Do you often neglect to send thank-you letters? Do you normally write a short note rather than a lengthy letter when you send a resume?

IF YES: Individuals who receive hundreds of letters from job seekers report similar problems with most letters they read. These problems can be corrected by following a few simple organization and content rules. Letters that don't pass the 5- to 10- second test tend to include several of these 16 errors:

1. Looks unprofessional in form, structure, and design.
2. Addressed to the wrong person or sent to the wrong place.
3. Does not relate to the employer's knowledge, interests, work, or needs.
4. Includes spelling, grammatical, and punctuation errors.
5. Uses awkward language and the passive voice.
6. Overly aggressive, assertive, boastful, hyped, and obnoxious in tone.
7. Self-centered rather than job- or employer-centered.
8. Poorly organized, difficult to follow, or wanders aimlessly.
9. Unclear what they are writing about or what they want.
10. Says little about the individual's interests, skills, accomplishments, or what they expect to achieve in the future.
11. Fails to include adequate contact information.

12. Dull, boring, and uninspired.
13. Too long.
14. Poorly typed.
15. Produced on cheap and unattractive paper.
16. Lacks information on appropriate follow-up actions.

In other words, many letters are just poorly written; they make negative impressions on readers. Letters that avoid these errors tend to be read and responded to. Make sure your letters are free of such errors!

TIPS: Several principles of effective advertising can be adapted to business writing and the job search. Indeed, the advertising analogy is most appropriate for a job search since both deal with how to best communicate benefits to potential buyers and users. These principles should assist you in developing your creative capacity to get what you want through letter writing.

Job search letters should be written according to the key principles of good advertising copy. They should include the following principles:

1. Catch the reader's attention.
2. Persuade the reader about you, the product.
3. Convince the reader with more evidence.
4. Move the reader to take action (invite to interview – not hire).

Form, style, content, production, and distribution all play important roles in communicating these persuasive elements in your letters.

Your letters should represent **you** – your personality, your credibility, your style, and your purpose. Start by asking yourself these questions **before** organizing and writing your letters:

- What is the **purpose** of this letter?
- What are the **needs** of my audience?
- What is a good opening sentence or paragraph for grabbing the **attention** of my audience?
- How can I maintain the **interest** of my audience?
- How can I best end the letter so that my audience will be **persuaded** to contact me?
- How much **time** should I spend revising and proofing the letter?
- Will this letter represent my **best professional effort**?

After writing your letter, review these questions again. But this time convert them into a checklist for evaluating the potential effectiveness of your letter:

- Is the **purpose** of this letter clear?
- Does the letter clearly target the **needs** of my audience?
- Does the opening sentence or paragraph grab the **attention** of my audience?
- Does the letter state specific **benefits** for the reader?
- Does the letter sustain the **interest** of my audience?
- Will the letter **persuade** the reader to contact me?
- Have I spent enough **time** revising and proofreading the letter?
- Does the letter represent my **best professional effort**?

Since your letters are a form of business communication, they should conform to the rules of good business correspondence:

- Organize what you will say by outlining the content of your letter.
- Know your purpose and structure your letter accordingly.
- Communicate your message in a logical and sequential manner.
- State your purpose immediately in the first sentence and paragraph.
- End by stating what your reader can expect next from you.
- Use short paragraphs and sentences; avoid complex sentences.
- Punctuate properly and use correct grammar and spelling.
- Use simple and straightforward language; avoid jargon or slang.
- Communicate your message as directly and briefly as possible.

Always keep in mind what you want your audience to do in reference to your job search:

- Pay attention to your message.
- Remember you.
- Take specific actions you want taken.

BARRIER #86
Send resumes and letters to the wrong places

QUESTIONS: Are you uncertain to whom you should address your resume and letters? Do you sometimes send your correspondence to "To Whom It May Concern" or "Dear Sir"? Do you primarily direct your correspondence to human resources or personnel? Do you have difficulty following up your resumes and letters because you don't know who received and read it?

IF YES: If you don't know who has your resume and letter, how will you follow up on your correspondence and ask for an interview? Too often candidates blindly send a resume and cover letter with little thought about the follow-up process – the most critical step to getting the interview. Without a proper follow-up, you may never hear from the employer. When you call to follow up on your resume and letter, you indicate your interest in the job as well as have an opportunity to refresh the employer's memory about you. If all goes well, he or she will take another look at your resume and possibly invite you to an interview based upon your follow-up call.

TIPS: Most personnel and human resources departments do not make hiring decisions. They may announce vacancies, process paperwork, handle benefits, and hire for positions within their departments, but most do not hire for positions in other departments. You need to research the organization and find out **who makes the hiring decisions** in your occupational area and then address your communication to that individual. The person who usually has the power to hire is found in an operational unit that has the actual hiring need. This also is the person, or persons, who will interview candidates. You will waste your time and effort by sending an unsolicited resume and letter to personnel or human resources.

Always try (make a phone call) to get the name of a specific person to whom you should address your, resume, letter, and follow-up phone call. When you call, ask the following question: *"Could you tell me to whom I should address my resume and letter?"* However, if you are unable to get a name, or if your inquiries result in instructions to *"just send it to Personnel or Human Resources,"* send your correspondence to the required department. Avoid standard anonymous salutations such as "Dear Sir/Madam" or "To Whom It May Concern." I prefer leaving the salutation off altogether and go directly from your return address at the top to the body of your letter. Do follow up within five days by calling the company and asking about your candidacy. When you call, ask them the following question about your resume and letter: *"Did you receive my resume and letter which I sent last week? When do you an-*

ticipate interviewing candidates and making a hiring decision?" Then indicate your interest in the position and ask if you could interview for it. Whatever you do, don't send another copy of your resume and letter. Employers know they are receiving multiple submissions, and they dislike such uncreative follow-up methods.

BARRIER #87
Include the wrong information or exclude important information

QUESTIONS: Are you uncertain what to include or exclude on your resume? Do you start writing your resume by writing "Resume" at the top? Have you included personal information on your resume? Should you include references on your resume? If an employer asks for your salary history, will you put it on your resume?

IF YES: Most resume and letter writers are unclear what to include or exclude on their resume. Much of this problem relates to understanding the purpose of a resume and letter. Should they summarize your work history? Should they provide a quick biography of who you are? If you don't understand the purpose of these documents, you are likely to include all kinds of irrelevant information as well as negative cues about you that will quickly kill your candidacy. The **purpose** of a resume and job search letters is to **get a job interview** which, in turn, should result in getting a job offer. Consequently, you want to include just enough information about yourself to persuade the reader to take enough interest in you to invite you to a job interview. Like good advertising copy, your resume and letters should immediately grab the employer's attention and move him or her to action – contact you for an interview.

TIPS: When writing your resume, avoid including any extraneous information that does not support your objective or communicate your qualifications to employers. Remember, you are not writing your resume to your mother, family, spouse, significant other, or a close friend. This is not an obituary summarizing everything you are or did in the past. The first thing to leave off your resume is the word "Resume"; it's obvious what it is. Avoid including your height, weight, age, sex, religion, health, politics, names and ages of children, spouse's occupation, parent's occupation, and other personal information that is not a bona fide job qualification. I've even come across a resume in which the candidate crossed out "single" and hand-wrote "married"! Also, do not include references or salary history/requirements. Apply this simple guiding inclusion/exclusion principle for packing a suitcase: *"When in doubt, throw it out!"* Your focus should be on communicating just enough information about your qualifications so the employer will be interested enough to invite you to a job interview.

What should be included and omitted in your cover letters? This question depends on your purpose and your audience. If you are responding to a vacancy announcement or a job posting, you need to address the stated requirements for submitting an application. This usually involves a resume and sometimes information on your "salary requirements."

Use the following general guidelines when trying to decide what to include or omit in your letters:

Things you should include:

- Positive information that supports your candidacy.
- Information on your skills, abilities, strengths, accomplishments, interests, and goals.
- Examples of your productivity and performance.
- Benefits you can offer the reader.
- A daytime contact telephone number and email address.

Things you should omit:

- Any extraneous information unrelated to the position, the employer's needs, or your skills.
- Any negative references to a former employer, your weaknesses, or the employer's organization and position.
- Boastful statements or proposed solutions to employer's problems.
- Salary requirements or history.
- References.
- Personal information such as height, weight, marital status, hobbies – information that should not appear on a resume.

BARRIER #88
Use the same resume and letters for different employers

QUESTIONS: Do you write one resume and send it to different employers? Do you basically use the same cover letter in response to different jobs?

IF YES: Different employers have different needs which should be addressed with different resumes and letters. If you use the same resume and cover letter in response to different positions, you will fail to respond to the specific needs of employers. Remember, employers are trying to hire someone who is the perfect **fit** for their requirements.

TIPS: Try to customize as much as possible your resume and cover letter in response to a position. If you are responding to a job posting, read the position description carefully and respond to each of the requirements with examples of your skills, abilities, and/or accomplishments. If, for example, the positions requires five years of progressive experience and you have such experience, be sure to mention that experience on your resume as well as emphasize it in your cover letter. If the position requires excellent marketing capabilities, let the reader know about your marketing accomplishments. Whenever possible, provide statistics relating to your performance. Examples and numbers relating to outcomes or accomplishments impress most employers. Make sure the objective on your resume directly relates to the needs of the employer.

One of the best ways to respond to a job posting is to use the classic "T" letter, which shows that you have the specific qualifications the employer is looking for by outlining step-by-step your qualifications in reference to the employer's stated requirements. Page 146 includes an example of such a "T" letter. Such a letter also can substitute for a resume. Again, the goal here is to provide just enough information to persuade the reader to contact you for more information as well as invite you to a job interview. "T" letters are powerful ways of doing so.

BARRIER #89
Fail to tell your story

QUESTIONS: Do you primarily focus on listing individual jobs and education background on your resume? Do you have difficulty summarizing who you really are in terms of your past accomplishments and

"T" Letter: Responding to Classified Ad

16 Bella Vista Place
Cincinnati, OH 45206
April 16, 20___

Ms. Cecily Dorfmann
Vice President, Human Resources
Nair Industries
257 Vine Street
Cincinnati, OH 45202

Re: Sales Manager, <u>Cincinnati Enquirer</u>, April 12

Dear Ms. Dorfmann:

As a Sales Manager, I have planned and scheduled direct sales programs and trade shows with consistently profitable results. Here is a list of my qualifications as they relate to your requirements for the position of Sales Manager:

<u>Your Requirements</u>	<u>My Qualifications</u>
2 years Direct Sales Management (Self-contained sales region)	Over 7 years aggressive direct sales management (experience as proven by opening 8 area offices which escalated regional sales average to #1 position among 200 offices.
Individual Sales Experience	Dynamic individual sales success proved by exceeding all sales goals for 18 months and reaching "Top ½%" among 250.
Excellent Verbal and Written Communication Skills	Exceptional communicator as demonstrated by over 40 major group presentations, writing "direct sales" promotional materials and column (reaching 11,000) and 3-day demonstrations at 22 national trade shows.
Problem Solving and Strategic Planning Skills	Excellent problem solver and strategic planner indicated by structuring daily control meetings for staff of 25 resolving problem of "peak time" business loss (increased 35%)
Marketing and Corporate Office Experience	Strong marketing experience (4 years) at corporate office level, proven skills in creating innovative team format and realigning 35 inside-outside sales/support staff to generate 15% sales increase to $3.5MM.

Enclosed is a resume that lists other accomplishments that may be of interest to you.

I look forward to meeting with you to explore the use of my talents to support the growth of your company. I will call on Wednesday, April 21, to schedule an interview at your convenience.

Sincerely,

Susan Ariani

Susan Ariani
Enclosure

future goals? Are you uncertain how to develop a series of memorable two-minute stories about your work life?

IF YES: While most job seekers communicate difference pieces of information about themselves to prospective employers, few of them can put together a coherent story about themselves. We each have stories about ourselves that can communicate to others our purpose and what we are especially talented at doing. These stories emphasize our goals, motivated patterns of skills, abilities, and accomplishments. They identify us as someone who is especially good at doing _____ and who should be hired because you will likely develop similar stories of accomplishments with a new employer.

The best candidates know how to tell compelling stories about themselves in reference to the employer's needs. They are adept at telling and re-telling stories about what they have done, can do, and will do in the future. These stories appear in their resume and letters and are articulated during job interviews.

TIPS: Ask yourself what are the five most memorable stories about your accomplishments that will likely impress potential employers? Can you tell each of these stories within two minutes? Begin developing a set of two-minute stories that should be represented on your resume and in letters as well as shared during your job interviews. Focus on stories that demonstrate your pattern of accomplishments. For example, instead of telling a prospective employer that you graduated from XYZ university with a B.A. in psychology, tell the interviewer why you decided to study psychology and how it relates to your career goals, including the job for which you are interviewing.

These five books can help you develop some great stories for writing your resume and preparing for the job interview:

- *The Art of Self-Promotion: Tell Your Story, Transform Your Career*
- *LinkedIn: Tell Your Story, Land the Job*
- *Tell Me About Yourself*
- *The Story of You: And How to Create a New One*
- *Tell Stories Get Hired*

BARRIER #90
Fail to follow up resumes and letters

QUESTIONS: Do you send a resume and letter and then wait to be called for an interview? Are you uncertain what you can do to get a prospective employer to contact you after he gets your resume and letter? Do you try to follow up your resume and letter by re-sending the same correspondence? Have you ever called an employer and then failed to send what you said you would send?

IF YES: Follow-up is the key to getting interviews and job offers. However, few job seekers ever follow up on their resumes and letters. If you fail to follow up your resume and letter, chances are you may never hear from an employer. When you follow up, you have a chance to get additional information about the position, conduct a screening interview, express your interest in the position and employer and move your application to the top of the pile. Many employers will make a special effort to read your resume and letter because of your follow-up actions. Most important of all, you will be remembered because of your interest in the position. In fact, employers like to hire individuals who indicate they are interested in a position and want to work for the employer.

Some job seekers have a bad habit of telling employers they will call them or send them something by mail, email, text, or fax, but they fail to do what they say they will do. If you want to make a bad impression on a prospective employer, don't follow through with what you say you will do.

TIPS: Once you send resumes to prospective employers, be sure to follow up within 48 hours after they receive your resume. If the employer has received many resumes during this time period, your telephone call or email will remind him or her who you are and your interest in the position. Take, for example, the cover letter on page 149. Notice the follow-up statement that appears in the third paragraph of this letter. In this case, the candidate lets the employer know that he will be calling on a particular day to inquire about his candidacy. With this statement, he effectively asks permission to talk about the position over the telephone. When you let the employer know you will be calling, be sure to make that follow-up call. If not, you may be seen as someone who does not follow through.

Cover Letter With Follow-Up Statement

2842 South Plaza
Chicago, Illinois 60228
March 12, 20___

David C. Johnson
Director of Personnel
Bank of Chicago
490 Michigan Avenue
Chicago, Illinois 60222

Dear Mr. Johnson:

The accompanying resume is in response to your listing in the Chicago Tribune for a loan officer.

I am especially interested in this position because my experience with the Small Business Administration has prepared me for understanding the financial needs and problems of the business community from the perspectives of both lenders and borrowers. I wish to use this experience with a growing and community-conscious bank such as yours.

I would appreciate an opportunity to meet with you to discuss how my experience will best meet your needs. My ideas on how to improve small business financing may be of particular interest to you. Therefore, I will call your office on the morning of March 17 to inquire if a meeting can be scheduled at a convenient time.

I look forward to meeting you.

Sincerely yours,

Joyce Pitman

Joyce Pitman
pitmanj@mymail.com

I prefer using the phone for doing this follow-up. A phone call also may give the employer an opportunity to conduct a telephone screening interview. Don't be too pushy at this stage. Use a low-key professional approach. Assuming you are able to get through to the person who received your resume, ask about your resume and the position:

- Hi, this is Emily Orlando. I'm calling in reference to my resume which I sent to you on June 3rd.
- Did you receive it?
- I know you're busy, but did you have a chance to review it yet?
- Do you have any questions at time?
- As I mentioned in my cover letter, I'm very much interested in this position, especially given my recent work at Rogers and Associates which focused on developing a new financial planning program for college graduates. I would love to have an opportunity to meet with you to discuss my work and how my experience might best contribute to your new programs designed for college students. Could we meet soon?

Notice how this conversation line moves from a polite *"Did you receive my resume?"* question to stressing the individual's key strength in reference to the employer's hiring need. Most important of all, this individual closes this follow-up call with an action statement – a request to interview for the job. While this is a moderately assertive approach, it is very targeted and professional. Although the employer may not wish to interview this individual right now, he or she may remember the candidate, re-read her resume, and put her at the top of the interview list. Being **remembered and prioritized** are two of the most desirable outcomes of such a resume follow-up call.

If you are unable to get directly through to the person to conduct this follow up conversation, be sure to access his or her **voicemail**. As I note with my co-author Neil McNulty in *The Quick 30/30 Job Solution*, voicemail may become your most important job search tool. We outline in detail how you can best use voicemail in your job search, including many effective sample messages. A good time to leave voicemail is after closing hours, when you're almost certain to get to a voice recording. Also, keep in mind that many busy people have two voicemails – a general voicemail box and a private voicemail box. Whenever possible, try to get the phone number for the private voicemail box and leave a compelling call-back message relating to your follow up.

8

Interviews, Communication, and Character

"The interview is the most critical stage of the job search. No interview, no job, and no paycheck. Preparation is the key to acing the job interview."

BARRIER #91
Unprepared for a telephone screening interview

QUESTIONS: If a employer called you today to conduct an interview over the telephone, would you feel unprepared to ace that interview? Have you assumed you'll just deal with a call from the employer if and when it occurs? Do you feel uncomfortable answering critical interview questions over the telephone?

IF YES: Before inviting candidates to job interviews, employers will conduct telephone screening interviews. If, for example, they have a list of 10 prospective candidates, many employers will want to reduce the number of candidates who will be invited to a job interview to three. They do this by calling each candidate and asking them a variety of questions for both screening them in and out of a face-to-face job interview.

TIPS: Since the consequence of a telephone screening interview is very important – determines whether or not you go on to a series of face-to-face job interviews – be sure to prepare well for this interview. In fact, this type of interview can happen any time – when you are in the middle of a meeting, when you are in hurry to go some place, or when you just stepped out of the shower. If you know you will be called at home, be

151

sure to prepare the telephone area for such a call. Include a file that has copies of correspondence you've sent to various employers and refer to that correspondence when you get called. Compile a list of questions you want to ask during this interview and keep it handy so you can quickly refer to those questions. Throughout the phone interview, try to sound as energetic and enthusiastic as possible. Keep in mind that the person at the other end will be trying to assess both verbal and non-verbal communication cues to determine whether or not to invite you to a job interview. Your grammar, tone of voice, pitch, completeness of answers, and vocalized pauses will all be scrutinized during this screening interview. And be sure to ask for a job interview as you close the telephone conversation. You might say something similar to this:

> I'm really interested in learning more about this position and your company and how my skills and accomplishments can best benefit your operation. Would it be possible for us to meet during this coming week?

This "is it possible" question opens the door for a job interview. If the response is that they are not ready to start interviewing, follow up this question with two other questions: *"When do you anticipate making a hiring decision? If I don't hear by _____, would it be okay if I give you a call?"* By asking permission to follow up, you keep the door open to a possible job interview.

BARRIER #92
Sound dreadful over the telephone

QUESTIONS: Do you sound better in person than over the telephone? Do you sound enthusiastic? Do you need to improve your oral communications? Do you have a heavy accent? Do you feel uncomfortable talking to strangers over the telephone? Do you quickly run out of things to say to a prospective employer? Do you get nervous when someone calls you for a telephone screening interview and thus talk too fast or lose your train of thought?

IF YES: Many people sound terrible over the telephone, even though they may do okay in face-to-face encounters. Not only do they speak in incomplete sentences and use bad grammar, the tone and volume of their voice are enough to turn off the person at the other end of the line. When speaking with a potential employer over the telephone, keep in mind that you are being screened for your oral communication skills as well for as the content of your answers. If, for example, the job in question involves using the telephone, your telephone manner will be assessed. How do you sound? Are you likable? Do you appear to be energetic and enthusiastic? Do you talk in complete sentences and use correct language? Are you too aggressive or too passive? Are you difficult to understand because of a foreign accent or the vague or disorganized manner in which you answer questions? Overall, do you sound like someone a employer would like to spend an hour or two interviewing in person? You simply **must** do well on the telephone if you hope to be invited to a job interview.

TIPS: Ask someone you trust to give you honest feedback to assess your telephone skills. While a telephone interview can be stressful, try to relax (take a deep breath), focus on the questions rather than on yourself, smile, sit or stand up straight, and try to be enthusiastic with your answers and questions. Have a friend call you and ask you a series of questions an interviewer might ask about a potential job. Better still, have them record your conversation, and then listen to it together to see what you need to do to improve your telephone skills. You need to assess the verbal and nonverbal aspects of the conversation. How well did you answer each question? Did you emphasize your "story" – pattern of skills and accomplishments related to the needs of the employer? Were you friendly, professional, and inviting in how you answered each question? Did you ask thoughtful questions? Did you close with a request for a job interview? How did you sound? Do you have a pleasant sounding voice that is neither too loud or too soft, too high-pitched or too low-pitched? Did you use complete sentences, proper grammar, correct pronunciation, and avoid using jargon unrelated to the position?

BARRIER #93
Use negative terms

QUESTIONS: Do you often use such terms as *"can't," "didn't," and "wouldn't"* in conversations? Do you have a hard time keeping a positive attitude during your job search? When talking about previous employers and co-workers, do you sometimes talk about the bad times and what was "wrong" with them? Are you still angry about what happened to you in a previous job?

IF YES: When speaking with a potential employer, avoid using negative terms. Remember, employers want to hire positive individuals who will contribute positive outcomes to their organization. People who use negative terminology tend to have negative attitudes that can be corrosive to an organization. Whatever you do, never bad-mouth your former employer or co-workers. Using negative terms to explain your previous work experience will tend to backfire on you – it says more about you, your attitudes, and your state of mind than about the behavior of the people you characterize in such terms.

TIPS: Keep your language as positive as possible. You want both the content of your responses and the manner in which you phrase your answers to be positive. As you talk about your previous employer(s), try to cast them in as positive a light as possible. If you have some issues with a previous employer that made you angry, it's time to let go and get on with your life. Close that door for good. While you can't change the past, you can shape your future. Concentrate on those things that you can change. Your continuing anger will sabotage your job search since it will come out during interviews. Learn from what happened, turn what may have been a negative situation into a positive, and simply move on by both forgiving and forgetting it. No one wants to hire an angry, unforgiving, or vindictive individual who lives in the past. After all, if you talk negatively about a former employer, the prospective employer will assume that someday you'll talk that way about her. If you badmouth your former company, the employer will expect that one day you'll do the same to his company. If you have only negative remarks about your co-workers, he will question your ability to get along in his organization as well. In other words, you have little to gain – and much to lose – during the interview by venting frustrations about previous jobs.

Try to put on the most positive spin possible – honest, but not stupid – as you phrase your responses. Avoid negative words such as *"can't," "didn't," "wouldn't,"* and phrase your answers with positive words instead. Rather than say, *"I wouldn't want to travel more than 4-5 days per month,"* you could respond with a more positive, *"I would prefer to keep my travel to 4-5 days per month."* Practice being more positive in your day-to-day communication and you will find it will come to you more easily in an interview. Being positive in what you say generally reflects on your overall attitude. If you have a negative attitude, chances are you use negative terms. Individuals with a positive and enthusiastic attitude tend to use positive terms.

BARRIER #94
Fail to mend broken fences with previous employers

QUESTIONS: Do you have unresolved issues with previous employers that could affect your future job prospects? Would any of your previous employers give you a negative recommendation? Do you have some red flags in your background that you would like to remove?

IF YES: If you have ever been fired or "let go" because of problems on the job, you may have a big red flag that could prevent you from getting another job you really want. If a prospective employer checks with a previous employer and finds that you were a problem employee, he may be reluctant to take a chance with you. If, for example, you were caught stealing or engaged in sexual harassment, you have some real explaining to do. On the other hand, if you were caught up in some organizational changes, such as the fact that your boss left and was replaced by someone else who wanted a fresh start with new personnel, you should be able to explain the political facts of organizational life that negatively affected you.

TIPS: Whatever the case, take stock of your red flags and try to neutralize any that relate to questionable relationships and evaluations you had on previous jobs. You can do this by deliberately mending broken fences. If you are still angry about what happened, get over it by calling your previous employer and trying to mend those fences.

The truth is that most employers quickly get over their personnel problems as they move on to new personnel, and most wish their previous employees well. If they get called for a reference, they will tend to verify your employment status rather than say anything negative about you and your work habits. They do this in part because of legal implications – they could get sued for making disparaging remarks (although they might win that lawsuit, there are still costs involved) – and in part because they simply wish you well (even though you may not think so!).

Make that phone call and let your previous employer know what you have done since you left his employment. Try to find something positive to say about your experience working with him which you have subsequently applied to other jobs. Then inform him that you are in the process of looking for a job and ask him what he might say if someone asks him why you left his company or how he would assess your major strengths. By doing this, you will probably neutralize his response as well as be prepared to deal with any adverse recommendation.

The one question he is likely to be asked by a prospective employer is this: *"If you had to do it over again, would you hire this person?"* Without going into much detail, a simple *"Yes"* or *"No"* answer to this question can be very revealing. You want this person to say *"Yes"* or explain that they no longer have a position for which you are a good fit. Thank him for his time, and then follow up with a thoughtful letter and a copy of your resume. By doing this you may actually make an ally out of someone you thought was a potential enemy in your quest for a new job! You've effectively neutralized what was a red flag.

BARRIER #95
Violate email etiquette and writing rules

QUESTIONS: Do you often use email and text? Do you quickly compose and send messages without carefully proofreading them? Do you prefer sending email and texts rather than writing paper letters? Do you send emails to strangers? When asked to email a resume, do you attach it to a short note?

IF YES: Emails and texts can be double-edged swords – they are quick and easy to compose and send, and they can quickly kill your chances of getting a job! Indeed, some of the worst communication that takes places is via email and texts.

Many writers are simply lazy – they quickly compose messages that are filled with grammatical, spelling, and punctuation errors with little thought of composing the perfect letter. A letter is a letter is a letter, regardless of the medium for sending it – mail, fax, email, or text. There is no rule that forgives writers from making errors when they use email and text. When you make organizational, grammatical, spelling, and punctuation errors, you effectively tell the reader that they are not important enough for you to be literate, and that you are less than serious about this job. You also tell prospective employers that you have some literacy problems you will be bringing to the job. If you will be dealing with customers, you will let them know that the employer hires people with poor communication skills. What other errors do you make?

If you can't write a coherent and error-free email message or text, frankly, you don't deserve to be considered for a job. If that represents your best effort, everything else will probably be downhill on this job!

Don't assume employers want to receive unsolicited emails and texts. They get enough such unsolicited communication each day that consumes a great deal of their time deleting as junk mail. Chances are 95 percent of your unsolicited emails will never get opened and read. You would have a much better chance of getting your letter opened and read if you wrote a formal letter and sent it by snail mail. At least it would stand out from all the other correspondence that tends to go by email these days.

TIPS: When composing email, take your time and **proofread, proofread,** and **proofread**. Grammatical, spelling, and punctuation errors are simply unforgiving in all of your job search communications, including emails. If you have a habit of quickly and cryptically composing and sending email messages, it is time to break that bad habit and join the ranks of thoughtful and error-free communicators.

There's a time to send emails and texts. That time is when a prospective employer asks you to email a resume and letter or text him or her. Make sure your subject line, which will largely determine if your message gets opened and read, immediately grabs the attention of the recipient; keep it simple, such as "Resume you requested." If you are sending a resume, make sure you include a thoughtful cover letter. In fact, most job seekers forget to send a letter with their emailed resume. Instead, they often say the following:

See attached resume

Thanks for reviewing my resume

This is simple laziness on the part of job seekers who think this whole process should be quick and easy – get an email address, attach your resume, say five words, and hit the "send" button. Since you have a great opportunity to pitch your resume and candidacy, don't waste it with a cryptic "Here it is" message. Emailed resumes that will get the most attention are those that are accompanied by a thoughtful subject line and cover letter. Take your time to craft an error-free cover letter to accompany your emailed resume. In fact, many employers report it is the quality of the cover letter, rather than the resume, that results in inviting a candidate to a job interview.

BARRIER #96
Fail to respond properly to job postings

QUESTIONS: Are you uncertain how to best respond to a job posting? Do you primarily send a copy of your resume with a short note? Do you send your resume and letter "To Whom It May Concern" or to "Dear Sir"?

IF YES: Fewer than 25 percent of all job seekers land jobs through the advertised job market of classified ads, vacancy announcements, or job postings. But most job seekers do spend a disproportionate amount of their job search time responding to this job market with resumes and letters and then waiting to get a positive reply. **Waiting** often appears to be their main job search strategy! Few formulate effective responses to job postings or engage in the key activity for getting invited to a job interview – follow up by telephone. For them, sending resumes and letters in response to job postings is a relatively passive activity that involves little effort beyond forwarding copies of their resume to an addressee.

TIPS: Effective job seekers are very proactive and entrepreneurial. You can significantly increase your odds of getting job interviews from job postings by doing the following:

1. **Read the announcement carefully** so you understand exactly what the employer is looking for in the ideal candidate. Get ready to respond to it with the perfect resume and letter.

2. **Customize your resume** so it addresses the specific requirements outlined in the announcement. If you don't have the requisite qualifications, don't waste your time engaging in wishful thinking. Pass on this one and move on to other job announcements that appear more appropriate for your interests, skills, and abilities.

3. **Craft a thoughtful cover letter** that expresses your enthusiasm for the position, stresses your key qualifications in reference to the ad, and closes with a follow-up statement.

4. **If you don't have a name of a person** to whom to send your resume and letter, contact the company and request the name. With a name, you can personalize your letter as well as direct your follow-up call to a specific person and his or her private voice-mail. If you can't get a name, send your resume and letter to the designated address.

5. **Follow up at the time you say you will follow up.** When you follow up, ask for a job interview.

6. **Always use the telephone whenever possible.** If you have good telephone skills, you may be able to screen yourself in to a face-to-face job interview.

7. **Move on to other job postings.** This is a numbers game. The more jobs you apply for, the greater the chances of getting a job interview. For every 100 resume and letters you send out in response to job postings, don't expect more than two invitations to job interviews. If you only send out 10 resumes and letters, you may not get any responses.

BARRIER #97
Arrive late for the job interview

QUESTIONS: Do you start looking for the interview location on the day of the interview? Will you make excuses for arriving late for a job interview?

IF YES: Do you want to really make a bad first impression on a prospective employer? Just show up late for the job interview! In fact, many candidates have difficulty getting to a job interview on time. They fail to allow enough time to find the interview location. Once they arrive late, they give stupid excuses for their tardiness – the employer's directions were bad, got held up at home, they had car trouble, or they got lost.

TIPS: Once you are invited to the interview, ask if there is anything you should know about the location, such as parking, security, or entrances to the building. Also, get the phone number just in case you need to call in late because you get caught up in an unexpected traffic problem. After all, accidents, road blocks, and construction do happen. Locate the interview location the day before the interview by using www. mapquest.com or some other Internet-based locator program. If feasible, do a trial run to locate the place and to figure out how long it will take to arrive, find parking, and get into the building. Some places have security requirements which may take additional time. Whatever time you decide it takes, add an extra 30 minutes for the unexpected. Ideally, you should be at the office at least 10 minutes before the scheduled interview. This will allow you time to relax, pick up an literature on the company, and engage in some useful small talk with a receptionist or other people you meet in the waiting room. Always remember that you are being observed during this waiting period. Indeed, after you leave, the interviewer may ask the receptionist what he or she thought of you. In other words, be on time and be nice to everyone you meet regardless of their position!

BARRIER #98
Bring a friend or relative to the job interview

QUESTIONS: Do you plan to bring someone with you to the interview site? Will you introduce this person to the interviewer?

IF YES: This is big red flag. Only **you** are invited to the interview. And only you should show up at the door for the interview. If someone needs to drive you to the interview and has plans to be with you after the interview, make sure that person doesn't come near the employer. He or she needs to stay with the car or go elsewhere until after the interview. No parents, no spouses, no children, or no friends should ever accompany you to a job interview. The presence of such people raises questions about your ability to function on your own. If you bring a child, you indicate you probably have a day-care problem. If you bring a parent, you don't appear to be responsible for your own employment. If you bring friends, your ability to function on your own is in question.

TIPS: Only show **your** face at the interview site – not other faces!

BARRIER #99
Project a poor image

QUESTIONS: Are you uncertain what to wear to a job interview? Do you go to a job interview looking the way you normally look? Do some people stare at you because of your appearance?

IF YES: The old saying that *"You never have a second chance to make a good first impression"* is especially true in job hunting. After all, you are primarily dealing with strangers who don't have much time to get to know the "real you." They often make snap judgments based upon first impressions.

Indeed, most interviewers decide within the first 60 seconds – before you've had a chance to answer and ask questions – whether or not they like you and want to hire you. In fact, many employers boast that they usually know within the first minute – their gut feeling – whether or not the person being interviewed is right or wrong for the job. That means they primarily make their hiring decision based upon nonverbal cues – what you wear, how you smell, your smile and sparkle in your eyes, and how you look. You may think that is unfair, but that's the reality of hiring. Consequently, it's very important that you pay particular attention to how you dress, smell, and look, since these elements may be decisive factors in determining whether or not you will be invited to additional interviews and offered a job. If you don't make a positive impression in the first 60 seconds, the rest of the interview will be all about overcoming a difficult impression you initially made. Most candidates don't recover from such situations.

TIPS: Your attire and appearance should not be negative factors in the job interview. You should dress appropriately for the interview. Dress at least one step above the position for which you are interviewing. For example, if you are interviewing for a blue-collar job that requires a uniform, go to the interview in neat, clean, and casual attire. If you are interviewing for a professional position, wear a suit. Stay with conservative colors – navy blues and grays. If you are overweight, wear dark-colored and loose-fitting clothes that do not draw attention to your weight – stripes should always run up and down, not around. Try ahead of time to get information on the dress code for the company you are interviewing with.

Avoid wearing lots of flashy jewelry and using heavy perfumes or colognes. Make sure your hair is neat and your nails are clean and trimmed. If you are heavily tattooed, try to cover up your body art as much as possible. Minimize body piercings by removing any jewelry that accentuates the piercings.

For guidance on how to best dress in reference to the workplace, see the following books:

- *Dress Like the Fig Fish*
- *Dress to Impress*
- *Dressing Smart for Men*
- *Dressing Smart for Women*
- *First Impressions*
- *Leave Your Nose Ring At Home*
- *The New Professional Image*
- *You've Only Got Three Seconds*
- *Winning Image*

BARRIER #100
Fail to engage in productive small talk

QUESTIONS: Do you feel uneasy engaging in small talk with strangers? Are you relatively introverted? Do you have difficulty networking? Do you dislike the idea of making cold calls? Are you uncertain how to greet the interviewer and what to say during the first five minutes? Is your attention span constantly interrupted by obsession with social media on your smartphone?

IF YES: If you are introverted, it will take some effort to strike up conversations with strangers and network for information, advice, and referrals – the keys to networking in a job search. At the same time, you need to acquire small-talk skills in order make a good impression at the job interview. What you say during the first five minutes of the interview, which is often devoted to small talk, will set the tone for the interview.

TIPS: You can develop effective small-talk skills by following the advice of several communication experts who specialize in networking and small talk as well as following my tips for Barriers #28 and 79 on shyness and networking. These books will get you up and running with small talk and networking:

- *The Fine Art of Small Talk*
- *A Foot in the Door*
- *How to Talk So People Listen*
- *How to Talk to Anyone*
- *How to Work a Room*

- *The Little Black Book of Connections*
- *Masters of Networking*
- *Never Eat Along*
- *One Phone Call Away*
- *The Power to Get In*
- *The Savvy Networker*
- *Self-Promotion for Introverts*
- *Social Networking for Career Success*
- *Work the Pond*

BARRIER #101
Unable to talk intelligently about yourself in reference to the employer's needs

QUESTIONS: Do you feel uncomfortable talking about yourself to others? Are you primarily interested in talking about salary and benefits?

IF YES: Many job seekers are uncomfortable talking about themselves. After all, they have learned since childhood not to boast about themselves or appear self-centered. Tooting one's horn does not come naturally to most job seekers. However, some narcissistic job seekers love talking about themselves and letting others think they are "the smartest person in the room."

Remember, employers want to know what it is you can do for them – not what you want from them. One of the first interview questions, which is actually a statement, you are likely to encounter is this one:

Tell me about yourself.

Many job seekers respond to this statement by giving a chronology of their education and work history, much of which already appears on their resume. This is not what employers really want to hear, since they already have this information.

TIPS: When asked to talk about yourself, be sure to focus on the **employer's needs**. These needs relate to the goals of the organization and your record of accomplishments. Be ready to **tell your story** of what you have done, can do, and will do in the future for this employer. The employer needs to know what it is you are likely to do for him – **your pattern of performance**.

BARRIER #102
Talk excessively rather than engage the employer

QUESTIONS: Do you tend to talk a lot? When asked questions, do you tend to embellish them with lengthy answers? Do you sometimes interrupt others as well as not know when to stop talking? Are you socially awkward? Do you have social timing issues – don't know when to start talking or end a conversation, move on to another subject, or simply say goodbye and leave on a positive note? Do others find you somewhat awkward – the last one they invite to join them at socials?

IF YES: One of the major reasons employers say they reject candidates is that they talk too much. They find such excessive talk irritating and the individual difficult to disengage from. When asked a simple question, they go on and on. They sometimes reveal personal information that normally would be illegal to ask, such as their age, marital status, health, political affiliation, religion, and family situation. They may even make stupid statements, such as negative comments about previous employers and co-workers, reveal dogmatic and intolerant attitudes, confess red flags in their background, and try to become too friendly and intimate. Many prematurely talk about salary and benefits – ask early in the interview about pay and vacation time. In fact, many employers want to hear candidates talk about themselves, since what they say may reveal a great deal about their motivation, personality, character, and suitability for the job.

TIPS: Be careful what you say during the job interview. This is not the time to confess your sins or ramble on about your previous jobs and relationships. Be very careful in asking about salary and benefit – **always** let the interviewer raise this question first. Keep focused on what you should be doing throughout the interview – learning more about the employer and the job and communicating your qualifications to the interviewer. Give thoughtful and focused answers that repeatedly convey your strengths as they relate to the job. If you find yourself talking at length – for more than three minutes at a time – you may want to slow down and leave more room for a conversation exchange since you may be talking too much and thus losing the interest of your audience.

BARRIER #103
Lack a good command of the English language

QUESTIONS: Do you have difficulty speaking English? Do some people have problems understanding you? Do you need to improve your command of English? When writing English, do you make grammatical, spelling, and punctuation errors?

IF YES: Language can be a major barrier to employment in the United States. While this is a multicultural country, it is not very forgiving of non-English speakers in the workplace. If you can't read, write, and speak English, you are basically illiterate and uneducated in the American workplace. Some jobs don't require a good command of English. Most of these are low-paying blue-collar jobs in agriculture, construction, food service, manufacturing, and landscaping – jobs that are disproportionately occupied by recent immigrants with a limited command of both oral and written English. If you have difficulty reading, writing, and speaking English, your career opportunities will be limited to low-paying jobs that also tend to have a high turnover rate.

TIPS: Learn to read, write, and speak English so you can advance your career. There's no excuse for not learning acceptable workplace English. You'll find numerous opportunities to learn English. Many churches offer free ESOL (English Speakers of Other Languages) classes, and most community colleges offer similar fee-based classes. Check with your local social services agency for information on English-language opportunities in your community.

If you are a native English speaker but have a poor command of your own language, especially bad grammar and spelling, check with your local high school (adult education) or community college for courses relating to improving English. Also, you may want to take a public speaking course or join Toastmasters International (www.toastmasters. org) that will help you organize your thoughts and deliver strong presentations. Also, do more reading, which will help improve your knowledge of English.

BARRIER #104
Exhibit irritating and disgusting habits

QUESTIONS: Do you bite your nails? Do you pick your nose or clean your ears in public? Do you clip your nails in public? Do you pass gas and make other irritating sounds in public? Do you smoke or chew tobacco? Do you chew gum? Do you use your cell phone in public as well as keep an eye and ear on it while engaged in conversations with others? Do you sometimes talk with your mouth full? Do you talk loudly and interrupt others?

IF YES: Employers want to hire and promote individuals who fit into their organizations, which means getting along well with other employees. Some job seekers exhibit disgusting habits both during the job search and on the job that can kill their candidacy and hold them back from getting ahead on the job. These behaviors include biting nails, picking nose, pulling hair, cleaning ears, trimming nails, cleaning teeth, coughing, clearing throat, blowing nose, applying makeup, or passing gas. Most are things one might do in the privacy of a bathroom or bedroom, even outside the view of close relatives and intimate friends.

Other less obnoxious but still irritating habits may relate to using your cell phone in public, talking loudly, laughing uncontrollably, talking excessively, touching others, interrupting conversations, standing too close to others, being too assertive and obnoxious, having bad breath, chewing gum, making inappropriate jokes and comments that embarrass others, talking with your mouth full, and failing to observe dining etiquette.

TIPS: Most people are unaware that their behaviors can offend others and label them as socially maladjusted. If you engage in any of these irritating and disgusting habits, you need to get some frank feedback on your behavior as well as a social makeover. Begin by asking a relative or close friend if there are things you do, especially any quirky behaviors, that might bother others. For starters, give them some of our examples. Get a good book on etiquette and read it thoroughly. Try these books for starters and then begin making the necessary changes in your behaviors:

- *Emily Post's Etiquette*
- *Etiquette for Dummies*
- *Everyday Etiquette*
- *Letitia Baldridge's New Manners for New Times*

BARRIER #105
Show little interest in the job or employer

QUESTIONS: Do you primarily focus on answering questions rather than asking questions during a job interview? Do you try to avoid eye contact with interviewers? Do you recline in the chair or seat from which you are being interviewed? Do you wait to hear from the interviewer rather than take certain follow-up actions within 48 hours of completing the interview?

IF YES: Employers want to hire candidates who are interested in working with them. If you are relatively passive throughout the interview, lack energy and enthusiasm, talk about salary and benefits, fail to ask questions, and just wait to hear from the employer after the interview, you probably appear to be disinterested in the job. Employers try to read candidates' interests and motivations both verbally and nonverbally. If you ask the killer question *"What do you do here?,"* you reveal that you've not done your homework by researching the organization and thus you indicate a lack of interest in the job. If you can't spend 10 minutes researching the organization on the Internet in preparation for the interview, why would an employer want to invest time and money hiring such a disinterested individual?

TIPS: Candidates who appear energetic and enthusiastic as well as ask thoughtful questions about the employer and the job are perceived to have a high level of interest. These candidates also engage in several nonverbal listening behaviors that indicate interest to the interviewer:

1. Maintain good eye contact.
2. Occasionally nod in agreement.
3. Smile when appropriate.
4. Sit with a slight forward lean toward the interviewer.

But the ultimate indication of interest in the job takes place at the closing of the interview and within 48 hours of finishing the interview. Be sure to close the interview by **summarizing** your understanding of the position and letting the interviewer know you are very interested in the position, if indeed you are. Ask when you might hear from him or her about the next step in the hiring process. Then, within 24 hours, write a nice thank-you letter in which you express your genuine appreciation for the opportunity to interview for the position and reiterate your continuing interest in the job. Within five days, call the employer and let him or her know that you are still interested in the position. In the end, your closing statement and follow-up actions may be decisive in getting the job offer. Never underestimate the power of a thoughtful thank-you letter!

BARRIER #106
Fear rejection

QUESTIONS: Are you sometimes reluctant to contact people for fear of being rejected? Do you expect to be turned down for a job interview or passed over for the job? Do you take rejections personally, as an indication of failure?

IF YES: Fear of rejections is often the most important self-imposed barrier to finding employment. Many job seekers prematurely limit their job search because they have difficulty handling rejections.

Let's face it. Few people can maintain the same level of energy, enthusiasm, and motivation throughout a three- to six-month job search. It's especially difficult when they encounter numerous rejections along the way. Indeed, the number one problem most job seekers encounter and have difficulty dealing with is rejections. Accustomed to being successful in other aspects of their lives, they find a job search can be very ego-deflating and depressing. In fact, most people can handle three rejections in a row, but four, five, six, or seven rejections are difficult to deal with. Faced with a string of rejections, many job seekers become demoralized, cut back on their job search activities, or just go through the motions of looking for a job by sending out more resumes and letters in response to job postings.

TIPS: There are certain things you can do to keep yourself focused and motivated. First, treat rejections as part of the game. You can't get acceptances before acquiring numerous rejections. Consider the typical job search which goes something like this:

No, No, No, No, No, No, Maybe, No, No, No, Yes, No, No, No
No, No, No, Maybe, No, Maybe, Yes, No, No, No, No, Yes, Yes

If you get disillusioned and quit after receiving four rejections, you will prematurely fail. You need to continue "collecting" more rejections in order to get an acceptance. In fact, I often recommend that individuals get up in the morning with the idea of collecting at least 20 rejections! You will eventually get acceptances, but you must first deal with many rejections on the road to success. How you handle rejections may largely determine how successful you will be in your job search, career, and life. If you identify what it is you want to do but cannot implement the necessary changes because you fear rejection, you will be going nowhere with your future.

Second, reward yourself after achieving certain goals. For example, let's say your goal this week is to send out 20 resumes, make 35 networking calls, and arrange four informational interviews. If you start on Monday and achieve these goals by Thursday, reward yourself by taking Friday off or go out for dinner at your favorite restaurant. Try to build a system of **rewards** related to specific goals so that you can occasionally celebrate successes. These little rewards will help keep you focused and motivated throughout your job search. Remember, this is a process that takes time and requires a positive approach to rejections.

BARRIER #107
Become discouraged and depressed

QUESTIONS: Are you sometimes discouraged by the lack of progress in finding a job? Do you at times get depressed and thus lack the will to go on making cold calls, networking for job contacts, and applying for jobs? Do you have a hard time getting motivated to conduct a well-organized and purposeful job search? Do you get envious of others who seem to be more successful than you in finding a job?

IF YES: You're not alone. Most job seekers go through bouts of discouragement and depression. The job search has its highs (invited to a job interview) and lows (rejected for the job). It's difficult to remain energetic and enthusiastic when faced with the realities of rejections and uncertainties. As any good salesperson will tell you, making the sale is all about attitude, probabilities, and persistence. Salespeople are great believers in the power of positive thinking. They have to be, since they are constantly being rejected! Whatever you do, don't interpret rejections as personal failures. Rejections and uncertainties are all part of the job search game. Everybody gets them, but only a few people know how to best deal with them. They constantly get up, dust themselves off, and continue down the road they have charted. They often see a silver lining in what appears to be a negative outcome. They put the past behind them – that's history – and focus on shaping their future. Through dogged persistence they prevail in making the sale. In your case, that sale is the perfect job you've been looking for. It's out there, but you must keep focused and motivated as you pursue your goals.

TIPS: If you become depressed and find it difficult to get motivated and keep active in your job search, take a few days off and engage in some useful volunteer work to recharge your batteries. Helping other people deal with their problems – be it housing, hunger, employment, illness, or death – will give you a different perspective on life. Chances are it will provide a fresh perspective on your situation and help motivate you to get back on track with your job search. Indeed, changing your environment by associating with different people and situations can be very refreshing. It will help you renew your focus and enthusiasm for conducting a well organized job search.

BARRIER #108
Lie about your past

QUESTIONS: When asked about your weaknesses, do you avoid telling the truth? When asked about potential red flags that appear on your resume, do you lie? Are there certain secrets about yourself that you don't want a prospective employer to know?

IF YES: A lot of lying goes on in the job search, especially on resumes and during job interviews. Many job seekers believe they have to stretch the truth or come up with false credentials and deceptive stories in order to get the job.

But the old adage that *"The truth will set you free"* now faces a new electronic age where there is no place to hide. Lying about your past to a prospective employer is risky business these days, since employers can easily do inexpensive background checks on everything from your employment record to your criminal and credit history. If you are caught lying during the interview process, you won't be offered the job. If you are hired and later found to have lied on your resume or during the interview, you will probably be fired.

TIPS: While you should always tell the truth, there is no rule that says you have to confess your sins, tell the whole truth in excruciating detail, volunteer your weaknesses, and share your secrets. Concentrate on the **needs of employers**. Tell your story. Focus on what's especially right about you – **your strengths**. After all, employers want to hire your strengths, even though they know they will probably inherit some weaknesses. You also want to be a person of **good character**. Individuals who have a pattern of lying or shading the truth eventually will be discovered, because they lack good character. Their **pattern** of lying and deception will eventually surface on the job.

BARRIER #109
Exaggerate your performance

QUESTIONS: Do you make up things that aren't really true, manufacture performance statistics, or tell stories that can't pass close scrutiny? Do you make statements about yourself that are less than accurate? Do you try to exaggerate your credentials because you fear you may not have enough going for you? Do you make self-serving performance statements that could blow up in your face if forced to give evidence – proof of performance – to verify those statements?

IF YES: Many job seekers don't really lie on their resumes or during interviews, but they live on the edge by exaggerating the facts. For example, if a candidate says she increased productivity by 35 percent during the first year on her last job, that would be an impressive statistic. However, if the interviewer decided to seek clarification by asking how the candidate arrived at that number, she might have trouble identifying the methodology that accounted for that statistic, especially if a company of 1,000+ employees had an overall 35 percent increase in productivity. Did she stretch the truth by taking credit for everyone's effort? How did she separate her contribution from that of others? Does she normally appropriate the work of others into her own performance statistics? What was really included in her performance appraisal for that year?

TIPS: Be honest in what you say and do. Take credit for those things you can measure as being a product of your efforts. But more importantly, focus on what you did to help your boss and co-workers achieve results.

The most valuable employees are those who give credit to others for what they do. They always try to make their boss look good rather than try to take credit for themselves. They develop a **reputation** for being an important team player who is always dependable – they are the person employers turn to when they need to get things done. Such people earn a stellar reputation as the quiet, loyal, competent, dependable, and reliable employee. Many of these workers never have to look for a job because the jobs come to them. Employers know who these stars are and they want to hire them away from the competition. When you become such an honest, competent, and employer-oriented worker, you will achieve a unique level of success where you may never again need to conduct a traditional resume-driven job search.

BARRIER #110
Attend job fairs unprepared

QUESTIONS: Have you neglected to attend job fairs or career conferences? Have you attended a job fair but felt unprepared to talk with employers? Are you aware that job fairs can be serious job hunting groups – some employers actually interview and hire at job fairs! Do you want to learn more about how you can effectively use job fairs in your job search?

IF YES: Many job seekers miss out on some of the best opportunities to meet employers, network for job leads, and interview for positions. These are found at job fairs and career conferences. Some job fairs are restricted to particular occupations and groups – information technology, health care, nurses, teachers, hospitality, construction, government, military, and security clearances. Career conferences are usually sponsored by a single employer or recruiting firm and attendance is by invitation only. You can get information on upcoming job fairs by surveying display ads in newspapers (usually the Sunday edition) or checking websites. Listings of upcoming military job fairs, for example, can be found at www.corporategray.com, www.taonline.com/MilitaryJobFairs, and www.vetjobs.com.

TIPS: You should keep the following nine tips in mind when planning to attend a job fair:

1. **Check to see if you qualify for the job fair.** There are different types of job fairs. Some job fairs are open to the general public and involve many different types of employers. These general job fairs are sometimes sponsored by a single company that is opening a new business and needs to recruit hundreds of people, such as a large hotel and conference center, sports arena, or an amusement park. Occasionally job fairs specialize in a particular skill or occupational area, such as high-tech, computer skills, clerical skills, or the construction trades. Organizations servicing different population groups, such as women, minorities, people with disabilities, and ex-offenders, often sponsor job fairs. And still others may be organized for government-related jobs and the intelligence and security communities.

   Transitioning military personnel and veterans have numerous opportunities to attend job fairs – both on-site and virtual (Internet-based) job fairs. Most military job fairs are open to all members of the military as well as veterans. A typical such job fair may include 50 to 100 employers and be attended by several hundred individuals who will soon be separating from the service. Veterans who are looking to change civilian employers may also attend these job fairs. Other military job fairs may be restricted to JMOs, officers, noncommissioned officers, and individuals with top secret security clearances.

   Special career events, such as career conferences sponsored by a single company, may be by invitation only.

2. **Be sure to pre-register for the job fair.** Some job fairs require you to pre-register for the event – not just show up at the door. Others only require registration at the door. One of the registration requirements is to submit a resume which, in turn, is entered into a resume database. This database enables employers attending the job fair to review the resumes online before and after the job fair.

3. **Plan ahead.** Prior to attending the event, try to get a list of companies that will be attending. Research several of the companies on the Internet. Discover what they do, who they employ, and what is particularly unique or different about them.

When you go the job fair, you will have some knowledge of those employers you want to meet. Better still, you'll impress the representatives when you indicate you know something about what their company does. You'll avoid asking that killer question, *"What do you do?"* Being prepared in this manner also means you will be more at ease in talking with employers, because you have some common ground knowledge for engaging in an intelligent job-oriented conversation.

4. **Be prepared to interview for the job.** Since some employers will actually interview candidates, don't assume a job fair is merely a casual get-together to just meet employers. Prepare for a job fair in the same way you would prepare for a job interview – dress appropriately, bring a positive attitude, be enthusiastic and energetic, anticipate questions, prepare your own questions, and observe all the verbal and nonverbal rules for interview success.

5. **Bring copies of your resume to the job fair.** Since you will be meeting many employers at the job fair as you circulate from one table or booth to another, your calling card is your resume. A good rule of thumb is to bring 25 to 50 copies of your resume to the job fair. Many job fairs also provide copying services, just in case you need to make more copies of your resume. If employers are interested in you, they will want to see your resume. Best of all, they will give you instant feedback on your qualifications. In many cases, they will interview you on the spot, asking questions you may be unprepared to answer! So make sure you write a terrific resume as well as bring enough copies for every employer you are interested in meeting. Anticipate being asked questions that normally arise during a formal job interview.

6. **Dress appropriately.** Job fairs are places where first impressions are very important. Be sure to dress as if you were going to a formal job interview – conservative and neat. Remember, you are meeting representatives of employers, and some encounters may turn into actual interviews in the representative's booth.

7. **Prepare a 30-second pitch or story about who you are and what you can do for an employer.** Your 30-second pitch should tell an employer who you are and what skills and experience you have that should be of interest to the employer. Tell them why they should consider interviewing and hiring you.

8. **Expect the unexpected.** Many first-time job fair attendees are surprised and unprepared to respond to prospective employer's questions. As a result, they make mistakes that could negatively affect their employment prospects and future income. For example, don't be shocked to encounter this question: *"What are your salary expectations?"* or *"What kind of salary are you looking for?"* Be very careful how you respond to this killer inquiry, which is primarily designed to quickly screen you in or out of further consideration. Not prepared for this question, some attendees stammer and then blurt out a specific figure that may be too low or too high. At this point in your job search, your answer should always be something like this: *"I'm open at this stage. Could you tell me more about the job and what it normally pays for someone with my qualifications?"* This puts the salary ball in the employer's court, which is where it should always be. Remember the old poker saying – *"He who reveals his hand first loses the advantage."* As you'll see later when I examine salary negotiations, salary is always the last thing you discuss **after** you have received a job offer. **Never** discuss salary specifics at a job fair.

9. **Follow up your contacts within 48 hours.** Job fairs are all about networking with employers. If you're interested in an employer and you've had a chance to meet a representative and get his or her name and business card, be sure to follow up with a phone call and/or email within 48 hours of your meeting. Time is of the essence since he or she may not remember you in a few days. This communication will remind the individual of your continuing interest and may result in a formal job interview with other company representatives.

BARRIER #111
Commit numerous interview sins

QUESTIONS: Do you get nervous before going into a job interview? Are you uncertain how to answer certain questions? Do you feel uncomfortable talking about salary? Do you need to know more about asking thoughtful questions and properly closing an interview?

IF YES: Many of the barriers addressed thus far come together during a face-to-face interview. Indeed, job seekers make numerous interview errors, many of which employers think are "unbelievable." Like resume and letter errors, interview sins can quickly knock you out of the competition. Unlike many other job search mistakes, interview errors tend to be unforgiving. This is the time when first impressions count the most.

Employers have both positive and negative goals in mind. On the positive side, they want to hire someone who can do the job and add value or benefits to their organization. On the negative side, they are always looking for clues that tell them why they should **not** hire you. After all, you are probably another stranger who makes inflated claims about your competence in the hope of getting a job offer. It's not until you start performing on the job that the employer gets to see the "real you" and discover your patterns of behavior. In the meantime, the employer needs to be on his or her guard looking for evidence that you may be the wrong person for the job. Make a mistake during the job interview and you may be instantly eliminated from further consideration. Therefore, you must be on your very best behavior and avoid the many common mistakes interviewers report that interviewees often make in face-to-face interviews:

1. **Arrives late to the interview.** First impressions really do count and they are remembered for a long time. Arrive late and you've made one of the worst impressions possible! Indeed, regardless of what you say or do during the interview, you may never recover from this initial mistake. Employers wonder *"Will you also come to work late?"*

2. **Makes a bad impression in the waiting area.** Treats receptionists and other gatekeepers as inferiors – individuals who may have important input into the hiring process when later asked by the employer *"What was your impression of this candidate?"* Caught reading frivolous materials – *People Maga-*

zine – in the waiting area when company reports and related literature were readily available.

3. **Offers poor and unacceptable excuses for behavior.** Excuses are usually red flags indicating that a person is unwilling to take responsibility and do the work. Here's a killer excuse for arriving late for a job interview: *"I got lost because your directions weren't very clear."* Goodbye! Other classic excuses heard during job interviews include:

- *I forgot.*
- *It wasn't my fault.*
- *It was a bad company.*
- *My boss was a real jerk.*
- *The college wasn't very good.*
- *I can't remember why I did that.*
- *No one there appreciated my work.*
- *I didn't have time to visit your website.*
- *I'm not a job hopper – I'm getting lots of experience.*

4. **Presents a poor appearance and negative image.** Dresses inappropriately for the interview – under-dresses or over-dresses for the position or the time of day. He or she may need to learn some basic grooming habits, from haircut and style to makeup and nails, or undergo a major makeover.

5. **Expresses bad, negative, and corrosive attitudes.** Tends to be negative, overbearing, extremely aggressive, cynical, and opinionated to the extreme. Expresses intolerance and strong prejudices toward others. Complains a lot about everything and everybody. Indicates a possible caustic personality that will not fit in well with the company. Regardless of how talented this person may be, unless he works in a cell by himself, he'll probably be fired within two months for having a bad attitude that pollutes the office and harms morale.

6. **Engages in inappropriate and unexpected behaviors for an interview situation.** Shows off scars, tattoos, muscles, or pictures of family. Flirts with the interviewer. Possibly an exhibitionist who may also want to date the boss and harass co-workers!

7. **Appears somewhat incoherent and unfocused.** Tends to offer incomplete thoughts, loses focus, and jumps around to unrelated ideas. Hard to keep a focused conversation going. Incoherent thought processes indicate a possible attention deficit disorder (ADD) problem.

8. **Inarticulate.** Speaks poorly, from sound of voice and diction to grammar, vocalized pauses, and jargon. Uses lots of *"you know," "ah," "like," "okay,"* and *"well"* fillers. Expresses a low-class or age-inappropriate street language – *"cool," "damn," "man," "wow," "awesome."* Not a good candidate for using the telephone or interacting with clients. Appears verbally illiterate or wired for failure.

9. **Gives short and incomplete answers to questions.** Tends to respond to most questions with *"Yes," "No," "Maybe,"* or *"I'm not sure"* when the interviewer expects more in-depth answers. Appears shallow and indicates a lack of substance, initiative, interest, and enthusiasm.

10. **Lacks a sense of direction.** Appears to have no goals or apparent objectives. Just looking for a job and paycheck rather than pursuing a passion or cause.

11. **Appears ill or has a possible undisclosed medical condition.** Looks pale, glassy-eyed, gaunt, or yellow. Coughs, sneezes, and sounds terrible. Talks about her upcoming surgery – within six weeks of starting the job! Suspects this person may have an illness or a drug and alcohol addiction.

12. **Volunteers personal information that normally would be illegal or inappropriate to ask.** Candidate makes interviewer feel uncomfortable by talking about religion, politics, age, family, divorce, sexual orientation, or physical and mental health.

13. **Emits bad or irritating smells.** Reeks of excessive perfume, cologne, or shaving lotion – could kill mosquitos! Can smell smoke or alcohol on breath. Strong body odor indicates personal hygiene issues. Has bad breath throughout the interview, which gets cut short by the employer for an unexplained reason!

14. **Shows little enthusiasm, drive, or initiative.** Appears to be just looking for a job and a paycheck. Tends to be passive and indifferent. No evidence of being a self-starter who takes initiative and solves problems on his own. Not sure what motivates this person other than close supervision. Indeed, he'll require lots of supervision or the company will have an employee with lots of play-time on his hands or the job will expand to fill the time allotted. He'll become the "job guy" who always says *"I did my job just like you told me,"* but not much beyond what's assigned. Don't expect much from this person, who will probably be overpaid for what he produces.

15. **Lacks confidence and self-esteem.** Seems unsure of self, nervous, and ill at ease. Lacks decisiveness in making decisions. Communicates uncertainly with such comments as *"I don't know," "Maybe," "I'm not sure," "Hadn't really thought of that," "Interesting question," "I'll have to think about that,"* or redirects with the question *"Well, what do you think?"*

16. **Appears too eager and hungry for the job.** Is overly enthusiastic, engages in extreme flattery, and appears suspiciously nervous. Early in the interview, before learning much about the company or job, makes such comments as *"I really like it here," "I need this job," "Is there overtime?," "What are you paying?," "How many vacation days do you give?"*

17. **Communicates dishonesty or deception.** Uses canned interview language, evades probing questions, and appears disingenuous. Looks like a tricky character who has things to hide and thus will probably be sneaky and deceptive on the job.

18. **Seems too smooth and superficial.** Dresses nicely, has a firm handshake and good eye contact, answers most questions okay, and appears enthusiastic – just like the books tell job seekers to do. But when asked more substantive *"What if"* and behavior-based questions, or requested to give examples of specific accomplishments, the candidate seems

to be caught off balance and stumbles, giving incomplete answers. Can't put one's finger on the problem, but the gut reaction is that this role-playing candidate is very superficial and will probably end up being the "dressed for success" and "coached for the interview" employee from hell!

19. **Appears evasive when asked about possible problems with background.** Gives elusive answers to red flag questions about frequent job changes, termination, and time gaps in work history. Such answers raise questions about the interviewee's honesty, credibility, responsibility, and overall behavior. Indicates a possible negative behavior pattern that needs further investigation.

20. **Speaks negatively of previous employers and co-workers.** When asked why she left previous employers, usually responds by bad-mouthing them. Has little good to say about others who apparently were not as important as this candidate.

21. **Maintains poor eye contact.** At least in America, eye contact is viewed as an indication of trustworthiness and attention. Individuals who fail to maintain an appropriate amount of eye contact are often judged as untrustworthy – have something to hide. Having too little or too much eye contact during the interview gives off mixed messages about what you are saying. Worst of all, it may make the interviewer feel uncomfortable in your presence.

22. **Offers a limp or overly firm handshake.** Interviewers often get two kinds of handshakes from candidates – the wimps and the bone-crushers. Your initial handshake may say something about your personality. Candidates offering a cold, wet, and limp handshake often come across as corpses! Bone-crushers may appear too aggressive.

23. **Shows little interest in the company.** Indicates he didn't do much research, since he knows little about the company and didn't have time to check out the company's website. Asks this killer question:

"What do you do here?"

24. Talks about salary and benefits early in the interview. Rather than try to learn more about the company and position as well as demonstrate her value, the candidate seems preoccupied with salary and benefits by talking about them within the first 15 minutes of the interview. Shows little interest in the job or employer beyond the compensation package. When the interviewee prematurely starts to talk about compensation, red flags go up again – this is a self-centered candidate who is not really interested in doing the job.

25. Is discourteous, ill-mannered, and disrespectful. Arrives for the interview a half hour late with no explanation or a phone call indicating a problem en route. Just sits and waits for the interviewer to ask questions. Picks up things on the interviewer's desk. Challenges the interviewer's ideas. Closes the interview without thanking the interviewer for the opportunity to interview for the job. Not even going to charm and etiquette school would help this candidate!

26. Tells inappropriate jokes and laughs a lot. Attempts at humor bomb – appears to be a smart ass who likes to laugh at his own jokes. Comes across as an irritating clown who says stupid and silly things. Will need to isolate this one to keep him away from other employees who don't share such humor and tastelessness.

27. Talks too much. Can't answer a question without droning on and on with lots of irrelevant talk. Volunteers all kinds of information, including interesting but sensitive personal observations and gossip the interviewer neither needs nor wants. Doesn't know when to shut up. Would probably waste a lot of valuable work time talking, talking, and talking and thus irritating other employees. Seems to need lots of social strokes through talk, which she readily initiates.

28. Drops names to impress the interviewer. Thinks the interviewer will be impressed with a verbal Rolodex of who he knows. But interviewers tend to be put off by such candidates who, instead, appear insecure, arrogant, and patronizing – three deadly sins that may shorten your interview from 45 minutes to 15 minutes!

29. **Appears needy and greedy.** Talks a lot about financial needs and compensation. When discussing salary, talks about his personal financial situation, including debts and planned future purchases, rather than what the job is worth and what value he will bring to the job. Seems to expect the employer is interested in supporting his lifestyle, which may be a combination of irresponsible financial behavior, failing to plan, living beyond his pay grade, and having bad luck. This line of talk indicates he probably has debilitating financial problems that go far beyond the salary level of this job.

30. **Closes the interview by just leaving.** Most interviewees fail to properly close interviews. How you close the interview may determine whether or not you will be invited back to another interview or offered the job. Never ever end the interview with this stupid and presumptuous closing prior to being offered the job: *"So when can I start?"* This question will finish off the interview and your candidacy – you're back to being needy and greedy! Also, don't play the pressure game, even if it's true, by stating *"I have another interview this week. When can I expect to hear from you?"* One other critical element to this close: send a nice thank-you letter within 24 hours in which you again express your appreciation for the interview and your interest in the job.

31. **Fails to talk about accomplishments.** Candidate concentrates on explaining work history as primarily consisting of assigned duties and responsibilities. When asked to give examples of her five major accomplishments in her last jobs, doesn't seem to understand the question, gives little evidence of performance, or reverts once again to discussing formal duties and responsibilities. When probed further for accomplishments, doesn't really say much and shows discomfort about this line of questioning.

32. **Does not ask questions about the job or employer.** When asked *"Do you have any questions?,"* candidate replies *"No"* or *"You've covered everything."* Asking questions is often more important than answering questions. When you ask thoughtful questions, you emphasize your interest in the employer and job as well as indicate your intelligence – qualities employers look for in candidates.

33. **Appears self-centered rather than employer-centered.** This will become immediately apparent by the direction of the answers and questions coming from the interviewee. If the candidate primarily focuses on employee benefits, he will be perceived as self-centered. For example, a candidate who frequently uses "I" when talking about himself and the job may be very self-centered. On the other hand, the candidate who talks about "we" and "you" is usually more employer-oriented. Contrast these paired statements about the job and compensation:

   "What would I be doing in this position?"
   "What do you see us achieving over the next six months?"
   or
   "What would I be making on this job?"
   "What do you normally pay for someone with my qualifications?"

34. **Demonstrates poor listening skills.** Doesn't listen carefully to questions or seems to have her own agenda that overrides the interviewer's interest. Tends to go off in different directions from the questions being asked. Not a very empathetic listener both verbally and nonverbally. Seems to be more interested in talking about own agenda than focusing on the issues at hand. Apparently wants to take charge of the interview and be the Lone Ranger. The job really does require good listening skills!

35. **Seems not too bright for the job.** Answering simple interview questions is like giving an intelligence test. Has difficulty talking about past accomplishments. Doesn't seem to grasp what the job is all about or the skills required. Seems confused and lacks focus. Should never have gotten to the job interview

but had a terrific looking resume that was probably written by a professional resume writer!

36. **Fails to know his/her worth and negotiate properly when it comes time to talk about compensation.** Job seekers are well advised to only talk about salary and benefits **after** being offered the job. If you prematurely talk about compensation, you may diminish your value as well as appear self-centered. Be sure to research salary comparables so you know what you are worth in today's job market (start with www.salary.com). Listen carefully throughout the interview and ask questions that would give you a better idea of what the job is actually worth. Stress throughout the interview your skills and accomplishments – those things that are most valued by employers who are willing to pay what's necessary for top talent. When you do start negotiating, let the employer state a salary figure first and then negotiate using salary ranges to reach common ground.

37. **Fails to properly prepare for the interview.** This is the most important mistake of all. It affects all the other mistakes. Indeed, failing to prepare will immediately show when the candidate makes a bad first impression, fails to indicate knowledge about the company and job, gives poor answers to standard interview questions, and does not ask questions. In other words, the candidate makes many of the mistakes outlined above because he or she failed to anticipate what goes into a winning interview.

TIPS: If you need help in preparing for the job interview, I recommend the following print and Internet resources:

Books

- *101 Dynamite Questions to Ask at Your Job Interview*
- *101 Great Answers to the Toughest Interview Questions*
- *250 Job Interview Questions You'll Most Likely Be Asked*
- *Adams Job Interview Almanac*, with CD-ROM
- *Best Answers to 202 Job Interview Questions*
- *Haldane's Best Answers to Tough Interview Questions*

- *I Can't Believe They Asked Me That!*
- *Job Interview Tips for People With Not-So-Hot Backgrounds*
- *Job Interviews for Dummies*
- *KeyWords to Nail Your Job Interview*
- *Nail the Job Interview*
- *Savvy Interviewing*
- *Win the Interview, Win the Job*
- *You Should Hire Me!*

Websites

- **Monster.com**   career-advice.monster.com
- **CareerOneStop**   www.careeronestop.org/jobsearch
- **JobInterview.net**   www.job-interview.net
- **Interview Coach**   www.interviewcoach.com
- **Quintessential Careers** www.quintcareers.com/intvres.html
- **The Riley Guide**   www.rileyguide.com/interview.html
- **The Ladders**   www.theladders.com/career-advice/
  interviewing
- **Vault.com**   www.vault.com/skills/interviewing.
  aspx

Most sites offer free interview tips and services, including Monster.com's "virtual interview." A few sites, such as InterviewCoach.com, charge consulting fees for assisting individuals in preparing for the job interview.

9

Salary, Benefits, Offers, and Follow-Up

"Knowing your worth and speaking money to power are skills few job seekers exhibit in today's job market. Once you master these critical skills, you'll be compensated for what you're really worth."

BARRIER #112
Prematurely talk about salary and benefits

QUESTIONS: Is *"How much does this job pay?"* one of the first questions you ask about a job? Are you the one who first brings up the question of salary and benefits? When asked about your salary expectations, do you normally state a specific figure?

IF YES: If you want to quickly kill your chances of getting the job or under-value your worth, just ask about salary and benefits early in the job interview or reveal your salary history before being interviewed. Remember, employers want to hire the best talent to perform the job. They also don't want to pay more than the going rate for someone with your talent.

At the same time, many job seekers appear needy and greedy when they ask about salary and benefits early on in the job interview. They also put themselves at a distinct disadvantage by prematurely revealing their salary expectations.

TIPS: Never talk about salary until you have been offered the job. Your preliminary research should give you a good idea of the going salary rate for someone with your experience and qualifications. That going rate should be the basis for your salary negotiation session, which should occur **after you have been offered the job**. If the employer asks you early in the interview about your salary expectations, this will be an opportunity for you to get additional salary information. Whatever you do at this stage, do **not** state a figure when asked this question. Instead, turn the question around and ask the following:

What do you normally pay someone with my qualifications?

Next, you should indicate that you need to learn more about the position before you can state your salary expectations. After all, you need to know what the job is **worth** before you can **value** it in terms of salary and benefits. If the employer persists in asking about your salary expectations, ask him the following:

Are you offering me the job?

If the answer is "no," continue discussing the position in order to get a better idea of what the job entails. Only after you have information on the work involved as well as information on salary comparables will you be ready to negotiate salary.

BARRIER #113
Reveal a great deal of personal information

QUESTIONS: Do you volunteer personal information when discussing your candidacy? Do you sometimes give employers too much information about yourself?

IF YES: Job seekers often talk too much and say the darnest things about themselves during job interviews. Indeed, employers have many "war stories" they share among themselves about what candidates said during job interviews. Many job seekers literally volunteer information that would be considered illegal for employers to ask, such as their age, marital status, religion, political affiliation, family planning situation, eldercare, and disabilities. Some even volunteer information about their health problems, financial difficulties, previous employment problems, and mental health issues. Employers are often amazed what interviewees are willing to confess to strangers who have the power to hire them! Indeed, this information makes many employers feel uneasy, since they know it's information that would be illegal for them to ask of candidates. However, it's not illegal to be in possession of such personal information.

TIPS: Watch what you say during the job interview. Don't talk too much and thus distract the interviewer from your professional qualifications. Whatever you do, don't volunteer personal information or anything that could be interpreted as negative information about yourself or your family. If your son Johnny is in jail for dealing drugs, your husband Bill is in alcohol rehab, your daughter Lizzy is pregnant by her 16-year old boyfriend, you are caring for your battered mother who has cancer, you flunked out of school, and you still hang out at biker bars, **don't** share any such information about what appears to be a totally dysfunctional family and challenging personal situation with a prospective employer. For an outside observer, your life is definitely out of control, and your job will most likely get subordinated to all this personal mess. If you've been divorced, are having an affair, or are gay, that's between you and your family or significant others – there is no need to share that information with an employer. If you are bipolar, keep it to yourself and make sure you take your medication. If you have financial problems, don't share them with an employer, who may interpret your situation as one of financial irresponsibility. You'll get no sympathy points for such stories that you think might help you get a job offer. Employers are not sympathetic social experimenters who want to hire needy people who stray off the success path. Instead, you've just given the employer another unbelievable candidate story he'll most likely share with his friends and colleagues who will probably have a good laugh at having dodged the bullet by not hiring someone with such a messy background!

BARRIER #114
Fail to listen carefully and respond appropriately

QUESTIONS: When being asked questions, do you tend to focus on trying to develop a good answer? Do you sometimes misunderstand what is being said?

IF YES: During a job interview you need to be a good listener for three major reasons. First, you want to get as much information about the company and job as possible so you can determine whether or not this is the right place for you. Second, you want to be able to respond to the interviewer's questions. Third, active listeners give interviewers positive nonverbal feedback that strengthens their candidacy.

TIPS: One of the best ways to become a good listener is to focus on the interviewer and what is being said rather than being preoccupied with yourself and how you are doing in the interview. If you focus on yourself, you will miss out on much of what is being said, you may seem disinterested in the conversation, and you may appear nervous and unenthusiastic. You'll most likely fail to ask thoughtful questions related to the conversation.

Listening is a learned skill. We learned to listen before we began our formal education – in fact, probably before we can even remember. Being a good listener takes effort. You can't lean back in your chair and listen passively and listen well. Listening requires active involvement. Good listening will produce several important outcomes. You will have the information needed to help you ask better questions, respond to questions more effectively, and eventually decide whether this is a job that is really fit for you. In order to do this, you should:

1. **Focus your attention on the interviewer and what he or she is saying.** Don't let your mind wander to such things as the strange or good-looking appearance of the interviewer, the photographs on the desk, your fears about not getting a job offer, or your plans for that evening or the weekend. We can listen and comprehend information about four times faster than the speaker is talking. Don't use that extra time to let your mind wander. Rather, concentrate on the message.

2. **Look beyond the personal appearance or mannerisms of the interviewer or any irritating words or ideas as you listen for content.** Don't let certain annoying words, ideas, or mannerisms of the interviewer so prejudice you that you can't listen objectively to what is being said.

3. **Try to listen for information and withhold evaluating the message until later.** This may be difficult to do, but it makes an important difference in what you get from the message. As we evaluate, our thoughts are on our reaction to the message, and thus we miss part of what the other person is saying.

4. **Give positive nonverbal feedback to the interviewer.** Nod
   in agreement occasionally if you agree, and smile occasionally if appropriate. Everyone likes to receive positive responses
   from others. Since most people interpret no response as a negative response, avoid an expressionless face. Your feedback is
   also likely to be interpreted as a sign of interest on your part.

If you try to concentrate on what is being said rather than how you are
doing, you will most likely create a good impression on the interviewer. Being other-directed with your nonverbal communication will make
you seem more likable and competent than candidates who remain
self-concerned and nervous throughout the interview.

BARRIER #115
Fail to ask questions

QUESTIONS: Do you go to a job interview without a list of questions
you want to ask? When asked during the interview if you have any
questions, do you say "no" or ask just one question?

IF YES: Always remember that a job interview should be a two-way
conversation involving a win-win situation. Both you and the interviewer want to learn more about each other in order to determine if
you want to work together. The interview should never be treated as a
game of winning or losing. Unfortunately, many job seekers approach
the interview as a contest – if they do the right things, especially give
answers to anticipated interview questions, they will win the job! Individuals who approach the job interview in this manner often flunk the
most important section of the interview – they fail to ask questions.
In fact, employers report that it's often the quality of the candidate's
questions that impressed them as much or more than their answers to
the interviewer's questions. Candidates who ask good questions do two
things that impress employers. First, they demonstrate their intelligence
– familiarity with the organization, their field, and major issues affect-
ing the company and productivity. Second, they indicate that they are
interested in both the company and the job.

TIPS: Always be prepared to ask good employer-centered rather than
self-centered questions during the job interview. You can jot these down

on a card or in the notes section of your smartphone, and refer to them when asked if you have any questions: *"Yes, I jotted down a few questions I wanted to make sure I asked."* The most impressive questions you can ask relate to issues facing the organization, possible solutions to problems, plans for the future, and the quality of personnel and operations. The least impressive questions, and ones that may have negative consequences, deal with self-centered issues relating to salary and benefits, including vacation days, sick leave, pension plans, and hours. Such questions should only be asked **after** you have received a job offer and are in the process of negotiating compensation. When you ask such questions during the job interview, you reveal your true motivations for seeking the position – money and other tangible rewards. Again, the employer wants to know what you can do for her and the organization.

BARRIER #116
Unable to give examples of your achievements

QUESTIONS: Do you have difficulty coming up with five examples of your work-related achievements? Do you feel uneasy about talking at length about each achievement?

IF YES: Employers are most impressed with candidates who can give examples and/or statistics relating to their previous achievements. They especially remember compelling stories relating to problems candidates solved – stories that include who, what, when, where, and with what consequences. While somewhat self-serving, the achievements should be related to how you took initiative, involved others, and achieved outcomes that benefitted your boss, co-workers, the organization, and clients.

TIPS: Develop five compelling stories that emphasize your achievements on previous jobs. Practice telling each story within two to three minutes. The stories should include who, what, when, where, and with what consequences for you, your boss, co-workers, the organization, and clients. Most of these stories should relate to achievements you already outlined in your resume and letters. For a good overview of achievement statements that can be developed into stories, see Appendix A of *Winning Letters That Overcome Barriers to Employment*. For an examination of how to engage in storytelling both during the job search and on the job, see *Tell Me About Yourself: Storytelling to Get a Job and Propel Your Career*.

BARRIER #117
Fail to close the job interview properly

QUESTIONS: Are you uncertain what to do at the end of the interview? Do you let the interviewer have the last word before you leave? Do you leave the interview thinking the interviewer might call you for another interview or extend a job offer, but you're really not sure?

IF YES: Already nervous from the whole interview process, many interviewees are just glad the interview is over, and they are happy to leave this stressful situation. That's one of the biggest mistakes you can make. Always close the interview properly.

TIPS: Assuming the interview has progressed to its final stage and you have asked questions about the organization, the job, and the work environment, you may breathe a sigh of relief. But you are not finished yet. Remember, you need to ask questions that will establish what you do from here. You do not want to go home and wait for weeks hoping to hear about this job.

Assuming you are still interested in the job, tell that to the interviewer. Ask when she (or the management team) expects to make a decision and when you could expect to hear. Then select the date a day or two after she has indicated a decision should be reached and ask, *"If I haven't heard from you by ___(date)___, may I call you?"* Almost always the interviewer will indicate you may call. Mark the date on your calendar and make certain you do call if you have not heard by then.

This is also a good time to ask the employer if there is any other information they need in order to act on your candidacy. If you still have questions concerning the job, you may want to ask the interviewer if there are two or three present or former employees you might talk to about the organization. He should provide you with the names, phone numbers, and emails. Be sure to contact them.

BARRIER #118
Fail to follow up interviews

QUESTIONS: After being interviewed, do you just wait to be called with a job offer? Do you need to develop stronger follow-up methods?

IF YES: It's very surprising how few candidates ever follow up on the job interview, including those who closed the interview properly and asked if they could call! The truth is that most job seekers are not very proactive. They think *"What will be, will be – they will call me if they truly want me."* As a result, most of them wait for the elusive call.

If you do nothing, you'll get nothing in return. Many employers report that it was the thank-you letter and/or phone call from a candidate that was decisive in offering him or her the job. All things being equal, which they often are at the final interview stage, the candidate who takes the initiative to follow up may get the job. Their follow-up actions, especially a thoughtful thank-you letter, indicate they are interested in the job, and confirm to the employer that this is the candidate they prefer working with.

TIPS: You need to take two follow-up actions after the interview. First, within 24 hours write a nice thank-you letter in which you express your sincere gratitude for the opportunity to interview for the position and reiterate your interest in the position. Within seven days after sending the thank-you letter, make a phone call to ask about your candidacy. Indicate again your appreciation for the interview and express once again your interest in the position. You may be pleasantly surprised with the response to these two follow-up actions. In many cases the result is a job offer!

BARRIER #119
Show a poverty of ideas and initiative

QUESTIONS: Do you lack three good ideas you can share with an employer? Do you lack an understanding of the problems facing the organization you're interviewing with? Is taking initiative one of your weaknesses?

IF YES: Employers want to hire self-starters who can take initiative, solve problems on their own, and require limited supervision. Individuals who have to be constantly supervised and told what to do throughout the day are a big drag on any organization.

TIPS: You need to view yourself as an entrepreneur. You're a business within a business. Your job is to contribute to the success of the organization. If you have to be told what to do, you really don't have a job. You're a standby worker who should be paid similarly to a day laborer – minimum wage. If you are uncertain what it is you should be doing, or if you have lots of down time, see your boss about your situation so you can redesign your job around your major strengths. Come up with a plan to revitalize that job. If you don't, you'll soon get bored with your lack of work and find yourself in trouble for not taking much initiative.

BARRIER #120
Fail to organize your references properly

QUESTIONS: Do you lack a good set of references who can speak to your major strengths? Have you failed to contact your references about your job search?

IF YES: Employers increasingly check your references to make sure you are who you say you are. Unfortunately, many job seekers make five major mistakes concerning their references:

1. They include too many self-serving references, such as relatives or close friends, who at best can only talk about their character. Volunteering such references may actually weaken a candidate.

2. They include questionable references who may not give a strong recommendation.

3. They fail to inform their references that they are looking for a job and ask whether they would be willing to give them a positive recommendation.

4. They list their references on their resume or in their cover letter rather than wait to provide them during the job interview.

5. They come to the interview with a portfolio of glowing but canned generic "To Whom It May Concern" letters written by so-called references on behave of the candidate, assuming these will substitute for an actual reference check.

TIPS: Be sure to include credible references who can speak about your accomplishments. These references should be able to verify what you have been telling the employer about yourself. Always contact your references and let them know you are looking for a job and ask whether you may use their name as a reference. Let former employers know they may soon be contacted by XYZ employer. Give them some background information about the job as well as an update on your job history. Better still, send them a copy of your resume for their reference.

You should never reveal your references until you are at the job interview. Take a list of your references to the job interview. If asked for references, give the interviewer a copy of your list. It should include the complete name, address, telephone number, and email address of at least three references. One may be personal, such as a minister or teacher who can talk about your character, but the others should relate to your work history.

BARRIER #121
Try to conduct a job search on your own

QUESTIONS: Do you try to conduct your job search on your own? Do you avoid seeking professional help?

IF YES: Many job seekers believe they can conduct a job search on their own. Just write a resume and send it to several employers; within a few days their phone should start ringing and they will be interviewed and offered a job. In reality, the job search is more complicated and unpredictable. While a resume is important for presenting qualifications to employers, the job interview is by far the most important element to landing a job. No resume, no interview; no interview, no job offer. At the same time, it may take three to six months to find the right job. During that time, most job seekers encounter numerous disheartening rejections that often diminish their energy and enthusiasm. My experience is that fewer than 20 percent of all job seekers can effectively conduct a job search on their own just by following the advice of career experts. The successful individuals tend to be self-starters who are very focused and motivated. The remaining 80 percent of job seekers can benefit from some form of assistance from career counselors, coaches, or a support group. Having someone to work with and share your experience with, including the inevitable ups and downs, can help immensely in moving your job search ahead. In fact, many job seekers can cut their job search time in half by working with a professional or support group. A career professional can be especially helpful at certain critical stages of your job search, especially in conducting a self-assessment, writing resumes, and preparing for interviews.

Since career planning is a big and largely unregulated business, you will occasionally encounter hucksters and fraudulent services aimed at taking advantage of individuals who are psychologically vulnerable, anxious, and naive. Many of these hucksters self-certify themselves, promise to locate jobs that pay more than your last one, and seal the deal by asking for up-front money – $500 to $15,000 – to find you a job. Lacking good shopping sense, engaging in wishful thinking, and vulnerable in this rather confusing and often depressing process, many job seekers fall for the false promises of these so-called employment experts.

TIPS: My advice is very simple: **Never** sign a contract before you read the fine print, get a second opinion, and talk to former clients about the **results** they achieved through the service. While most of these services are not free, there is no reason to believe that the most expensive services are the best services. In fact, you may get the same quality of services from a group that charges $300 versus one that costs much more. At the same time, free or cheap services are not necessarily as good as the more expensive services. While you often get what you pay for in this industry, you also may get much less than what you pay for! Again, before using any employment services or hiring an expert, do your research by asking for references and contacting individuals who have used the services.

Take, for example, public employment services. These services usually consist of a state agency which provides employment assistance as well as pays unemployment compensation benefits. Employment assistance largely consists of job listings and counseling services. However, counseling services often screen individuals for employers who list with the public employment agency. If you are looking for an entry-level job or a job paying $20,000 to $50,000, contact these services. However, most employers still do not list with them, especially for positions paying more than $50,000 a year.

Although the main purpose of these offices has been to dispense unemployment benefits, don't overlook them because of past stereotypes. The Workforce Investment Act of 1998 and the Workforce Innovation and Opportunity Act (WIOA) of 2014 have re-energized such services. Within the past 15 years, many of these offices have literally "reinvented" themselves for today's job market as American Job Centers (AJCs). Over 2,500 AJCs operate nationwide to help people find jobs, training, and answers to employment questions. You can find the AJC nearest you by visiting the locator section of the U.S. Department of Labor's gateway career website: www.careeronestop.org. These centers offer a wide range of employment services to veterans and the general public, including career and job information computer job search, computer resume service, state job banks, employment counseling, federal bonding program, interpreter/reader, job placement, job search workshops, resources, skills assessment, and worksite training.

Certified career professionals are experienced in working one-on-one with clients, with special emphasis on career assessment. They have their own professional associations. If you are interested in contacting a certified career professional for assistance, we advise you to first visit these websites for locating a career professional:

- **Association of Career Professionals**   www.acpinternational.org
- **The Career Experts**   www.thecareerexperts.com
- **Career Planning and Adult Development Network**   www.careernetwork.org
- **Career Thought Leaders**   www.careerthoughtleaders.com
- **National Board for Certified Counselors, Inc**.   www.nbcc.org
- **National Career Development Association**   www.ncda.org
- **PARW/CC**   www.parw.com

You also can find a great deal of professional career assistance through the U.S. Department of Labor's CareerOneStop website, which enables users to locate services within their communities:

www.careeronestop.org/LocalHelp/service-locator.aspx

Whatever you do, be a smart shopper for career planning and job search services. Proceed with caution, know exactly what you are getting into, and choose the best. Remember, there is no such thing as a free lunch, and you often get less than what you pay for. At the same time, the most expensive services are not necessarily the best. Indeed, the free and inexpensive career planning services offered by many community or junior colleges – libraries, computerized career assessment programs, testing, and workshops – may be all you need. On the other hand, don't be afraid to spend some money on getting the best services for your needs. You may quickly discover that this money was well spent when you land a job that pays 20 to 40 percent more than your previous job!

Whatever you do, don't be *"pennywise but pound foolish"* by trying to do your job search on the cheap. If you have difficulty writing a first-class resume, by all means contact a resume-writing pro who can put together a dynamite resume that truly represents what you have done, can do, and will do in the future. You can quickly find some of the best professional resume writing expertise by searching these three websites:

- **National Resume Writers' Association**   www.thenrwa.com
- **Professional Association of Resume Writers and Career Coaches**   www.parw.com
- **ResumeWriters**   www.resumewriters.com

BARRIER #122
Look for a job involving a long commute

QUESTIONS: Have you been tempted to take a job that involves a long commute? Do you dislike commuting to work? Do you need to figure how much a long commute will actually cost you each day?

IF YES: Be careful what you wish for. While some people can cope with the long commutes, especially if they use comfortable public transpor-tation, others quickly find the commute gets very old. In fact, it may have adverse effects on both your personal and professional lives.

At the same time, many employers are leery of candidates who will have to commute a long distance to work. Such individuals may soon tire of the commute and thus look for opportunities closer to home or try to work out a telecommuting arrangement. They also may become unreliable employees who at times will have difficulty getting to work – family emergencies, vehicle problems, or doctor/dentist appointments. Try as you may to convince a prospective employer that your long and expensive commute is "no problem" for you, all other things equal between two candidates, he or she will choose the one with the shorter commute. Be prepared for this potential objection to hiring you.

TIPS: Try as you may to rationalize a long commute to work, it is a problem on several fronts. First, it's increasingly expensive in an economy with rising energy costs. Can you, for example, afford to spend $25 to $60 a day commuting to work – the estimated cost of gasoline and parking for a 120-mile round trip commute each day? Second, do you want to spend an extra two to three stressful hours commuting to work each day? That adds up to 40 to 60 extra hours of road time each month – time that could be productively spent with your family or doing other things. Third, how long do you expect to stay with an employer who is located such a distance from your home? Would you be better off finding a job near your home or moving closer to the employer? As noted in Barrier #67, most people want to find a job within 30 minutes of home. For assistance in achieving that goal, check out the unconventional job search tips outlined in *The Quick 30/30 Job Solution: Smart Job Search Tips for Surviving Today's New Economy*.

BARRIER #123
Fail to involve your spouse or significant other in your decisions

QUESTIONS: Do you sometimes make important decisions without consulting your spouse or significant other? Have you gotten in trouble before for making decisions that should have involved others close to you?

IF YES: What do you think would happen if you came home one day and said, *"Honey, I got a new job and we're moving to Albuquerque!"* If you're like many other people, you're in big trouble for playing the Lone Ranger, especially since your decision affects other people's lives. If you want to grow old together, you better make your job search a joint team effort.

TIPS: Closely involve your spouse or significant other in your job search. If your job search involves making a major move, which could affect two jobs or careers, conduct your job search together. Not only will the process be easier since you'll be able to give each other mutual support, you'll maintain a good relationship as you both go job hunting.

BARRIER #124
Take the first job offered

QUESTIONS: Are you anxious to get a job? Are you likely to take the first one that is offered to you?

IF YES: Anyone can find a job, but finding the right job takes time. Unfortunately, many people who have been discouraged by rejections will take the first that is offered. That may be a big mistake, especially if it is not a good fit.

TIPS: Carefully assess any job offer. When offered a position, ask the employer for a couple of days to consider it. This is a common professional courtesy. During that time you need to ask yourself some important questions:

- Is it a job you will do well and enjoy doing?
- Does it give you the opportunity to pursue your interests and
- utilize your best skills?
- Will you be able to grow in this job and advance your career?
- Do you like the people you will be working with?

Also, take this time to check on any other jobs you are considering. Follow up on any that you are particularly interested in and let the employer know that you have a job offer elsewhere. This information may result in another offer from which you can compare and contrast. And don't forget to check on comparable salaries and compensation options since you still need to negotiate salary and benefits.

BARRIER #125
Take the first salary offered

QUESTIONS: Are you uncertain how to negotiate compensation? Are you afraid you'll lose the job if you don't accept the first salary offer? Do you feel the salary offered is non-negotiable?

IF YES: Except for entry-level salaries, most salaries are negotiable. In fact, most people are probably underpaid by 10 to 20 percent because they fail to negotiate their salary. But this is understandable in a culture where we are taught from a young age not to talk about other people's incomes. As a result, many job seekers are relatively "salary dumb," because they don't know what other people earn in similar positions. They also lack basic salary negotiation skills that could significantly increase their incomes.

TIPS: Learn to develop basic salary negotiation skills. I discuss these skills at length in three other books:

- *Get a Raise in 7 Days*
- *Give Me More Money!*
- *Salary Negotiation Tips for Professionals*

One of the most basic salary negotiation principles is to focus on **salary ranges** rather than a specific salary figure. Indeed, savvy salary negotiators always talk about salary ranges. They do so because ranges give them flexibility in the negotiation process. If, for example, the employer reveals his hand first by saying the job pays $75,000 a year, you could counter by putting the employer's figure at the bottom of your range:

> *Based on my salary research as well as my experience, I was thinking more in terms of $75,000 to $85,000 a year.*

By doing this, you establish **common ground** from which to negotiate the figure upwards toward the high end of your range. While the employer may not want to pay more than $75,000, he or she at least knows you are within budget. The employer most likely will counter by saying,

> *Well, we might be able to go $78,000.*

You, in turn, can counter by saying

> *Is it possible to go $81,000?*

As you will quickly discover in the salary negotiation business, anything is possible if you handle the situation professionally – with supports and flexibility. In this situation, you might have been able to negotiate a $6,000 increase over the employer's initial offer because you established common ground with a salary range and then moved the employer toward the upper end of your range because you had supports and professional appeal. But make sure you have done your homework, have valid salary comparables, and are not just engaging in wishful thinking.

Many employers will try to impress candidates with the **benefits** offered by the company. These might include retirement, bonuses, stock options, medical and life insurance, and cost of living adjustments. If the employer includes these benefits in the salary negotiations, do not be overly impressed. Most benefits are standard – they come with the job. So why negotiate something you're going to get anyway?

When negotiating salary, it is best to talk about specific dollar figures. But don't neglect to both calculate and negotiate benefits, which can translate into a significant portion of your compensation, especially if you are offered stock options, profit sharing, a pension, insurance, and reimbursement accounts. Indeed, many individuals in the 1990s who took stock options in lieu of high salaries with start-up high-tech firms discovered the importance of benefits when their benefits far outweighed their salaries; making only $30,000 a year, some of them became instant millionaires when their companies went public! The U.S. Department of Labor estimates that benefits now constitute 43 percent of total compensation for the average worker. For example, a $60,000 offer with Company X may translate into a compensation package worth $80,000; but a $50,000 offer with Company Y may actually be worth more than $100,000 when you examine their different benefits.

If the salary offered by the employer does not meet your expectations, but you still want the job, you might try to negotiate for some benefits which are not considered standard. These might include longer paid vacations, some flextime, and profit sharing.

BARRIER #126
Fail to get the job offer in writing

QUESTIONS: Have you accepted job offers that were not in writing? Were you ever surprised that the job did not turn out to be the same as the stated offer? Do you think you should get your next offer in writing?

IF YES: Some employees are surprised to discover the job they were offered was not the one they received. Indeed, considerable slippage between the promise and the performance can take place if you don't get the offer in writing. This could lead to misunderstandings, distrust, and feelings of betrayal because of so-called "broken promises."

TIPS: You should take notes throughout the salary negotiation session. Jot down pertinent information about the terms of employment. At the end of the session, before you get up to leave, summarize what you understand will be included in the compensation package and show it in outline form to the employer. Make sure both you and the employer understand the terms of employment, including specific elements in the compensation package. If you accept the position, be sure to ask the employer to put the offer in writing, which may be in the form of a letter of agreement. Do not ask for such a letter if you have not accepted the job. This document should spell out your duties and responsibilities as well as detail how you will be compensated. If your agreement includes incentivized pay, make sure it states exactly how your commissions or bonuses will work – how and when they will be paid, set up, and measured. For example, will you be paid at the end of each quarter or at the end of the year? Will you receive a flat bonus, such as $1,000, or a percentage of the sales from an income stream?

Ask the employer to email or fax you a copy of this document for your review. Let him know you'll get back with him immediately. This document should serve as your employment contract.

BARRIER #127
Forget to send thank-you letters to key people

QUESTIONS: Do you often forget to send thank-you letters? Do you know at least three people you should send thank-you letters to during your job search?

IF YES: As we noted in Tip #79, networks need to be built and nurtured. And prospective employers need to hear from you after the interview and before a job offer is extended. One of the keys to networking and getting a job offer is the thank-you letter. It communicates important values in today's busy and self-centered society – you are a thoughtful person who appreciates assistance and opportunities.

TIPS: Unfortunately, many networkers abuse relationships by using people without ever thanking them for their assistance. A simple thank-you letter, which takes no more than 15 minutes to complete, will discharge this important obligation as well as continue nurturing important relationships. The same is true about the job interview. If you want to be remembered as a thoughtful candidate, as well as have additional input into the hiring process, you should send a thank-you letter to the interviewer within 24-hours after completing the job interview.

Examples of numerous types of thank-you letters relating to the networking and interview processes can be found in my two letter-writing books:

- *201 Dynamite Job Search Letters*
- *Nail the Cover Letter!*

Index

Career Resources

THE FOLLOWING CAREER resources are available from Impact Publications. Full descriptions of each, as well as downloadable catalogs and video clips, can be found at www.impact publications.com. Complete the following form or list the titles, include shipping (see formula at the end), enclose payment, and send your order to:

IMPACT PUBLICATIONS
9104 Manassas Drive, Suite N
Manassas Park, VA 20111-5211
1-800-361-1055 (orders only)
Tel. 703-361-7300 or Fax 703-335-9486
Email: query@impactpublications.com
Quick & easy online ordering: www.impactpublications.com

Orders from individuals must be prepaid by check, money order, or major credit card. Since prices may change, please verify online at www.impactpublications.com before ordering. We accept telephone, fax, and email orders. Some titles available on GSA Schedule.

Qty.	TITLES	Price	TOTAL
Featured Title (GSA Schedule – Contract #GS-02F-0146X)			
_____ Overcoming Employment Barriers		$19.95	_____
Pocket Guides (GSA Schedule – Contract #GS-02F-0146X)			
_____ Anger Management Pocket Guide		$2.95	_____
_____ Military Personal Finance Pocket Guide		2.95	_____
_____ Military Spouse's Employment Pocket Guide		2.95	_____
_____ Military-to-Civilian Transition Pocket Guide		2.95	_____
_____ Quick Job Finding Pocket Guide		2.95	_____
_____ Re-Entry Employment & Life Skills Pocket Guide		2.95	_____
_____ Re-Entry Personal Finance Pocket Guide		2.95	_____
_____ Re-Entry Start-Up Pocket Guide		2.95	_____
_____ Re-Imagining Life on the Outside Pocket Guide		2.95	_____
Attitude, Motivation, and Inspiration			
_____ 7 Habits of Highly Effective People		$17.00	_____
_____ 17 Lies That Are Holding You Back		19.99	_____
_____ 30 Lessons for Living		16.00	_____
_____ 100 Ways to Motivate Yourself		15.99	_____
_____ The Art of Doing		16.00	_____
_____ Attitude Is Everything		16.99	_____
_____ Awaken the Giant Within		17.99	_____
_____ Breaking the Habit of Being Yourself		16.95	_____
_____ Change Your Attitude		16.99	_____
_____ Change Your Thinking, Change Your Life		22.00	_____
_____ Create Your Own Future		21.00	_____
_____ Do What You Love, the Money Will Follow		17.00	_____
_____ The Element: How Finding Your Passion Changes Everything		16.00	_____
_____ Finding Your Own North Star		15.00	_____
_____ Get the Life You Want		19.95	_____
_____ Goals!		19.95	_____
_____ How to Win Friends and Influence People		16.95	_____
_____ Magic of Thinking Big		15.99	_____
_____ The Power of Habit		16.00	_____
_____ The Power of Positive Thinking		15.99	_____
_____ The Purpose-Driven Life		16.99	_____

_____	Reinventing Your Life	17.00 _____
_____	The Secret	23.95 _____
_____	The Success Principles	19.99 _____
_____	Think and Grow Rich	18.95 _____
_____	What Should I Do With My Life?	18.00 _____
_____	What You're Really Meant to Do	27.00 _____
_____	Wishcraft: How to Get What You Really Want	16.00 _____

Reimagining a Life With Purpose

_____	Claiming Your Place At the Fire	$16.95 _____
_____	From Age-ing to Sage-ing	15.00 _____
_____	Life Reimagined: Discovering Your New Life Possibilities	16.95 _____
_____	Man's Search for Meaning	9.99 _____
_____	The Power of Purpose	17.95 _____
_____	Repacking Your Bags	17.95 _____
_____	Something to Live For	16.95 _____
_____	Your Best Life Ever	21.99 _____
_____	Your Life Calling: Reimagining the Rest of Your Life	16.00 _____

Mindfulness

_____	The Gifts of Imperfection	$14.95 _____
_____	Mindfulness: A Practical Guide to Awakening	25.95 _____
_____	Mindfulness for Beginners	21.95 _____
_____	Mindfulness for Dummies	26.99 _____
_____	The Mindfulness Solution	16.95 _____
_____	One-Minute Mindfulness	15.95 _____
_____	The Power of Now	15.00 _____
_____	Super Brain	15.00 _____
_____	Thrive	26.00 _____

Personal Finance

_____	9 Steps to Financial Freedom	$15.99 _____
_____	Money Book for the Young, Fabulous, and Broke	16.00 _____
_____	The Truth About Money	21.95 _____

Career Exploration

_____	50 Best Jobs for Your Personality	$19.95 _____
_____	100 Great Jobs and How to Get Them	17.95 _____
_____	150 Best Jobs for a Secure Future	17.95 _____
_____	150 Best Jobs for Your Skills	17.95 _____
_____	200 Best Jobs for Introverts	16.95 _____
_____	200 Best Jobs Through Apprenticeships	24.95 _____
_____	250 Best-Paying Jobs	17.95 _____
_____	300 Best Jobs Without a Four-Year Degree	20.95 _____
_____	America's Top Jobs for People Re-Entering the Workforce	17.95 _____
_____	Best Jobs for the 21st Century	19.95 _____
_____	Occupational Outlook Handbook	19.95 _____
_____	Progressive Careers	229.95 _____
_____	Top 100 Health-Care Careers	25.95 _____

Finding Jobs and Getting Hired

_____	The 2-Hour Job Search	$12.99 _____
_____	95 Mistakes Jobs Seekers Make...and How to Avoid Them	13.95 _____
_____	Change Your Job, Change Your Life	21.95 _____
_____	Encore Career Handbook	16.95 _____
_____	Getting a Job You Want After 50 For Dummies	22.99 _____
_____	Guerrilla Marketing for Job Hunters 3.0	21.95 _____
_____	Job Hunting Tips for People With Hot and Not-So-Hot Backgrounds	17.95 _____
_____	Knock 'Em Dead: The Ultimate Job Search Guide	16.99 _____

_____ No One Will Hire Me!   15.95   _____
_____ Overcoming Barriers to Employment   19.95   _____
_____ The Quick 30/30 Job Solution   14.95   _____
_____ Second-Act Careers   14.99   _____
_____ What Color is Your Parachute? (annual edition)   19.99   _____

Career Assessment

_____ Career Match $15.00   _____
_____ Discover What You're Best At   15.99   _____
_____ Do What You Are   18.99   _____
_____ Everything Career Tests Book   15.99   _____
_____ Gifts Differing   18.95   _____
_____ Go Put Your Strengths to Work   16.00   _____
_____ I Don't Know What I Want, But I Know It's Not This   15.00   _____
_____ I Want to Do Something Else, But I 'm Not Sure What It Is   15.95   _____
_____ Pathfinder   17.95   _____
_____ What Color Is Your Parachute Workbook   12.99   _____
_____ What Should I Do With My Life?   18.00   _____
_____ What Type Am I?   17.00   _____
_____ What You're Really Meant to Do   25.00   _____

Assessment Instruments (packages of 25)

_____ Barriers to Employment Success Inventory $63.95   _____
_____ Career Exploration Inventory   60.95   _____
_____ Job Survival and Success Scale   53.95   _____
_____ Transition-to-Work Inventory   57.95   _____

Resumes and Cover Letters

_____ 101 Best Resumes $20.00   _____
_____ 201 Dynamite Job Search Letters   19.95   _____
_____ Best Career Transition Resumes for $100,000+ Jobs   24.95   _____
_____ Best Cover Letters for $100,000+ Jobs   24.95   _____
_____ Best KeyWords for Resumes, Cover Letters, and Interviews   17.95   _____
_____ Best Resumes for $100,000+ Jobs   24.95   _____
_____ Best Resumes for People Without a Four-Year Degree   19.95   _____
_____ Blue-Collar Resume and Job Hunting Guide   15.95   _____
_____ Damn Good Resume Guide   11.99   _____
_____ Executive Job Search for $100,000 to $1 Million+ Jobs   24.95   _____
_____ Expert Resumes for Military-to-Civilian Transitions   18.95   _____
_____ Gallery of Best Resumes for People Without a Four-Year Degree   18.95   _____
_____ Haldane's Best Cover Letters for Professionals   15.95   _____
_____ Haldane's Best Resumes for Professionals   15.95   _____
_____ High Impact Resumes and Letters   19.95   _____
_____ Knock 'Em Dead Cover Letters   14.99   _____
_____ Knock 'Em Dead Resumes   14.99   _____
_____ Military-to-Civilian Resumes and Letters   21.95   _____
_____ Modernize Your Resume   18.95   _____
_____ Nail the Cover Letter   17.95   _____
_____ Nail the Resume!   17.95   _____
_____ Resume, Application, and Letter Tips for People
      With Hot and Not-so-Hot Backgrounds   17.95   _____
_____ Resume Magic   18.95   _____
_____ Resumes for Dummies   18.99   _____
_____ Savvy Resume Writer   12.95   _____
_____ Winning Letters That Overcome Barriers to Employment   17.95   _____

Networking and Social Media

_____ Branding Yourself $24.99   _____
_____ Dig Your Well Before You're Thirsty   16.95   _____

_____ How to Find a Job on LinkedIn, Facebook, Twitter, and Google+	20.00	_____
_____ How to Work a Room	15.99	_____
_____ Job Searching With Social Media for Dummies	19.99	_____
_____ Knock 'Em Dead Social Networking	15.99	_____
_____ LinkedIn for Dummies	24.99	_____
_____ The Little Black Book of Connections	19.95	_____
_____ Make Your Contacts Count	14.95	_____
_____ Networking for People Who Hate Networking	16.95	_____
_____ Never Eat Alone	27.00	_____
_____ The Power Formula for LinkedIn Success	16.95	_____
_____ Self-Promotion for Introverts	22.00	_____
_____ Social Media Job Search Workbook	39.00	_____
_____ Social Networking for Career Success	20.00	_____
_____ Social Networking for Introverts	22.00	_____
_____ Work the Pond	16.95	_____

Small Talk

_____ The Fine Art of Small Talk	$18.00	_____
_____ How to Be a People Magnet	18.00	_____
_____ How to Make People Like You in 90 Seconds or Less	11.95	_____
_____ How to Start a Conversation and Make Friends	15.00	_____
_____ How to Talk So People Listen	12.99	_____
_____ How to Talk to Anyone	16.95	_____
_____ Talking to Yourself	9.95	_____

Storytelling

_____ LinkedIn: Tell Your Story, Land the Job	$12.99	_____
_____ Tell Me About Yourself	24.95	_____
_____ Tell Stories Get Hired	19.95	_____

Interviewing

_____ 101 Dynamite Questions to Ask At Your Job Interview	$13.95	_____
_____ 101 Great Answers to the Toughest Interview Questions	12.99	_____
_____ Best Answers to 202 Job Interview Questions	17.95	_____
_____ I Can't Believe They Asked Me That!	17.95	_____
_____ Job Interview Tips for People With Not-So-Hot Backgrounds	14.95	_____
_____ KeyWords to Nail Your Job Interview	17.95	_____
_____ Knock 'Em Dead Job Interviews	14.95	_____
_____ Nail the Job Interview	17.95	_____
_____ Savvy Interviewing	10.95	_____
_____ Sweaty Palms	13.95	_____
_____ Win the Interview, Win the Job	15.95	_____
_____ You Should Hire Me!	15.95	_____

Salary Negotiations

_____ Get a Raise in 7 Days	$16.95	_____
_____ Give Me More Money!	17.95	_____
_____ Salary Negotiation Tips for Professionals	16.95	_____

Job Keeping and Revitalization

_____ How to Be a Star At Work	$15.00	_____
_____ Love 'Em or Lose 'Em	24.95	_____
_____ The One Thing You Need to Know	29.95	_____
_____ Overcoming 101 More Employment Barriers	19.95	_____
_____ What Your Boss Doesn't Tell You Until It's Too Late	13.95	_____
_____ Who Gets Promoted, Who Doesn't, and Why	14.95	_____

Ex-Offenders and Re-Entry Success

_____ 99 Days to Re-Entry Success Journal	$4.95	_____
_____ Best Jobs for Ex-Offenders	11.95	_____

_____ Best Resumes and Letters for Ex-Offenders   19.95 _____
_____ The Ex-Offender's 30/30 Job Solution   11.95 _____
_____ The Ex-Offender's Job Interview Guide   11.95 _____
_____ The Ex-Offender's New Job Finding and Survival Guide   19.95 _____
_____ The Ex-Offender's Quick Job Hunting Guide   11.95 _____
_____ The Ex-Offender's Re-Entry Assistance Directory   29.95 _____
_____ The Ex-Offender's Re-Entry Success Guide   11.95 _____

Addictions

_____ A to Z of Addictions and Addictive Behaviors $19.95 _____
_____ The Addiction Workbook   21.95 _____
_____ The Addictive Personality   15.95 _____
_____ Addictive Thinking   15.95 _____
_____ Alcoholics Anonymous: Big Book   14.95 _____
_____ Alcoholism and Addiction Cure   15.95 _____
_____ Breaking Addiction   14.99 _____
_____ Denial Is Not a River in Egypt   13.95 _____
_____ Ending Addiction for Good   14.95 _____
_____ A Gentle Path Through the Twelve Steps   18.95 _____
_____ How to Get Sober and Stay Sober   14.95 _____
_____ How to Quite Drugs for Good!   16.95 _____
_____ The Recovery Book   17.95 _____
_____ Sex, Drugs, Gambling, and Chocolate   16.95 _____
_____ Sober But Stuck   15.95 _____
_____ Stop the Chaos   15.95 _____

Anger and Conflict

_____ Anger and Conflict in the Workplace $14.95 _____
_____ The Anger Workbook   14.95 _____
_____ Angry Men   14.95 _____
_____ Angry Women   14.95 _____
_____ Beyond Anger: A Guide for Men   15.99 _____
_____ Controlling People   15.99 _____
_____ Of Course You're Angry   14.95 _____

Learning Disabilities and Mental Health

_____ ADD/ADHD Checklist $16.95 _____
_____ Bipolar Disorder   15.95 _____
_____ Complete Learning Disabilities Handbook   34.95 _____
_____ Delivered From Distraction   16.00 _____
_____ Driven to Distraction   15.95 _____
_____ Feeling Good Handbook   26.00 _____
_____ The Gift of Dyslexia   16.95 _____
_____ Learning Outside the Lines   15.99 _____
_____ Overcoming Dyslexia   17.95 _____
_____ Surviving Manic Depression   19.95 _____
_____ Taking Charge of ADHD   19.95 _____
_____ You Mean I'm Not Lazy, Stupid, or Crazy?   19.00 _____

Start and Manage a Business

_____ $100 Startup $23.00 _____
_____ 101 Small Business Ideas for Under $5,000   32.00 _____
_____ The $100,000 Entrepreneur   19.95 _____
_____ Business Plans Kit for Dummies (with CD-ROM)   34.99 _____
_____ Six-Week Start-Up   21.95 _____
_____ Small Business Start-Up Kit   29.99 _____
_____ Start Your Own Business   24.95 _____

Special Value Kits

_____ Discover What You're Best At Kit	$435.95 _____
_____ Job Finding With Social Media and Technology Kit	282.95 _____
_____ Learning From Successes and Failures Kit	1,059.95 _____
_____ Mindfulness for Refocusing Your Life Kit	297.95 _____
_____ New Attitudes, Goals, and Motivations Kit	411.95 _____
_____ New Military-to-Civilian Transition Kit	653.95 _____
_____ Overcoming Employment Barriers Kit	124.95 _____
_____ Overcoming Self-Defeating Behaviors and Bouncing Back Kit	245.95 _____
_____ Reimagining Life: Discovering Your Meaning and Purpose	203.95 _____
_____ Start Your Own Business Kit	316.95 _____
_____ Tony Robbins "Transform Your Life" Collection	189.95 _____

DVD Programs

_____ 135 Interview Answers	$169.95 _____
_____ 175 Resume Secrets	169.95 _____
_____ 207 Interview Techniques	169.95 _____
_____ Barriers to Communication and How to Overcome Them	129.95 _____
_____ Careers in the Nonprofit Sector	129.95 _____
_____ Common Job Interview Mistakes	99.95 _____
_____ Digital Communication Skills	129.95 _____
_____ E-Networking for Jobs	129.95 _____
_____ Get Hired and Go	599.95 _____
_____ Getting the Job You Really Want	995.00 _____
_____ Job Seeker: Interview Do's and Don'ts	169.95 _____
_____ Navigating the World of Social Media	108.00 _____
_____ Resumes: A How-to Guide	99.95 _____
_____ Soft Skills in the Workplace	149.95 _____
_____ STEM Careers in Two Years	389.95 _____
_____ What Will I Say at the Interview?	129.95 _____
_____ You're Fired!	149.00 _____

TERMS: Individuals must prepay; approved accounts are billed net 30 days. All orders under $100.00 should be prepaid.

RUSH ORDERS: fax, call, or email for more information on any special shipping arrangements and charges.

SUBTOTAL	_____
Virginia residents add 6% sales tax	_____
California residents add ____% sales tax	_____
Shipping ($5 +8% of SUBTOTAL)	_____
TOTAL ORDER	_____

Bill To:

Name_____ Title _____
Address_____
City _____ State/Zip _____
Phone ( )_____ (daytime)
Email_____

Ship To: (if different from "Bill To;" include street del. address).

Name_____ Title _____
Address_____
City _____ State/Zip _____
Phone ( )_____ (daytime)
Email_____

PAYMENT METHOD: ☐ **Purchase Order #**_____ (attach or fax with this order form)

☐ **Check** – Make payable to IMPACT PUBLICATIONS

☐ **Credit Card**: ☐ Visa ☐ MasterCard ☐ AMEX ☐ Discover

Card #																Expiration Date		
Signature										Name on Card (print)								

Overcoming Employment Barriers Kit

#7015 Addresses major employability issues for those lacking sufficient work experience, education, and skills as well as those with a history of job hopping, and incarceration. Can purchase separately. **SPECIAL: $124.95 for all 8 books.**

- *95 Mistakes Job Seekers Make and How to Avoid Them* $($13.95)
- *The Ex-Offender's New Job Finding and Survival Guide* ($19.95)
- *I Want to Do Something Else, But I'm Not Sure What It Is* ($15.95)
- *Job Hunting Tips for People With Hot and Not-So-Hot Backgrounds* ($17.95)
- *No One Will Hire Me!* ($15.95)
- *Overcoming Barriers to Employment Success* ($17.95)
- *Overcoming Employment Barriers* ($19.95)
- *Winning Letters That Overcome Barriers to Employment* ($17.95)

Job Finding With Social Media and Technology Kit

#8471 Update your career library by getting the latest inside scoop on how to conduct a powerful job search using social media. Can purchase each separately. **SPECIAL: $282.95 for all 14 books.**

- *The 2-Hour Job Search* ($12.99)
- *Branding Yourself* ($24.99)
- *Guerrilla Marketing for Job Hunters 3.0* ($21.95)
- *How to Find a Job on LinkedIn, Facebook, Twitter, and Google +* ($20.00)
- *Job Searching With Social Media for Dummies* ($19.99)
- *Knock 'Em Dead Social Networking* ($15.99)
- *LinkedIn for Dummies* ($24.99)
- *The Panic Free Job Search* ($15.99)
- *The Power Formula for LinkedIn Success* ($16.95)
- *Resumes for Dummies* ($18.99)
- *The Social Media Job Search Workbook* ($49.00)
- *Social Networking for Career Success* ($20.00)
- *The Web 2.0 Job Finder* ($15.99)
- *What Color Is Your Parachute?* ($19.99)

Ex-Offender Re-Entry Guides Collection

#6847 These five popular workbooks help ex-offenders effectively re-enter society and the workforce. Each workbook emphasizes taking responsibility, changing attitudes, and making smart decisions. Jam-packed with revealing examples, interactive tests, and insightful exercises. 128-144 pages each. 2009-2016. Can purchase separately at **$11.95 each. SPECIALS: Purchase all 5 re-entry guides (*Ex-Offender Re-Entry Guides*) for $57.95; 10 sets of all 5 guides for $493.00; 25 sets for $1,159.00; 100 sets for $3,697.00.**

- *Best Jobs for Ex-Offenders*
- *The Ex-Offender's 30/30 Job Solution*
- *The Ex-Offender's Job Interview Guide*
- *The Ex-Offender's Quick Job Hunting Guide*
- *The Ex-Offender's Re-Entry Success Guide*

SCAN ME